200,000 Snakes: On the Hunt in Manitoba

Life after cancer is not a 45-degree angle upwards. Pat's experience embodies the need to anchor yourself to the unknown, with style.

Matthew Zachary, Founder of Stupid Cancer and OffScrip Media

Pat Spain is that rare thing: a rationalist who still embraces the possible and knows that there are more things in heaven and earth than are dreamt of. A grown-up who has lost none of the childhood wonder and curiosity that makes the world magical. A scientist who keeps an open mind and rejoices in the fact that absence of proof is not proof of absence. There is nobody I'd want to travel with more to explore the wild side of our literally extraordinary planet. Buckle up and prepare for adventures.

Harry Marshall, Chairman and Co-Founder of Icon Films

I've heard Pat's stories in person, on TV, on weekly pandemic Zooms, and in front of one of the most demanding audiences there is: teenagers. But when you've got a living, breathing YouTube video like Pat Spain – who actually knows what it's like to go literally, biologically viral – the stories never get old, whatever the age. Pat's message is exactly what my teens – all the rest of us – want and need to hear. Be yourself unapologetically. What makes you weird makes you special. Love the people who love you for that. And cherish every moment you have while you've got it. It won't last forever.

Luke Kirkland, Award-Winning Librarian & Teen Department Head, Waltham Public Library

Titles in the On the Hunt series

200,000 Snakes: On the Hunt in Manitoba

or How I Found a New Beginning at the Bottom of a Giant Pit of Snakes

200,000 Snakes:
On the Hunt
in Manitoba

or How I Found a New Beginning at
the Bottom of a Giant Pit of Snakes

Pat Spain

6TH
BOOKS

Winchester, UK
Washington, USA

JOHN HUNT PUBLISHING

First published by Sixth Books, 2022
Sixth Books is an imprint of John Hunt Publishing Ltd., No. 3 East St., Alresford,
Hampshire SO24 9EE, UK
office@jhpbooks.com
www.johnhuntpublishing.com
www.6th-books.com

For distributor details and how to order please visit the 'Ordering' section on our website.

Text copyright: Pat Spain 2021

ISBN: 978 1 78904 648 9
978 1 78904 649 6 (ebook)
Library of Congress Control Number: 2021941985

A CIP catalogue record for this book is available from the British Library.

Design: Stuart Davies

UK: Printed and bound by CPI Group (UK) Ltd, Croydon, CR0 4YY
Printed in North America by CPI GPS partners

We operate a distinctive and ethical publishing philosophy in
all areas of our business, from our global network of authors to
production and worldwide distribution.

Contents

This book is for my wife, Anna Nguyen Spain. I still have no idea why you ever agreed to go to the aquarium with me, but I am so grateful every day for that remarkable lapse in judgment.

A disclaimer

My dog Daisy was the best. She loved hanging out in the backyard with my sister Sarah and me when we were playing hide-and-go-seek, catching bugs, or looking for arrowheads on the trails behind our house in Upstate NY. She would wait patiently at the base of any tree we climbed and chase away our neighbor's super scary dog (he ate a kitten once). She would also stand guard while I waited for the spider to crawl out of a crack in our chipped blue bulkhead cellar doors. It was huge, with green-metallic colored fur and red eyes, and Daisy would growl if I put my hand too close it. She was a white poodle mix with poofy fur and perpetually muddy feet. Also, Daisy could fly, sometimes wore a cape, and would occasionally speak with a Southern drawl.

I don't have schizophrenia and Daisy was not an imaginary friend – but she also didn't really exist. Despite never owning a dog as a child, I have honest, distinct memories of Daisy. Memories that go well beyond the stories my mom used to tell my sister and me about Daisy saving us from one tragedy or another. I also have detailed memories of being terrified, like heart-racing, nearly-in-tears fear the time Cookie Monster stole our shoes while we were wading in the creek catching crayfish and pollywogs. He would only give them back when we had the Count (who smelled like toothpaste) help us negotiate how many cookies it would take for each shoe, shoelace, and sock. Daisy ran back and forth from our house bringing with her a ransom of the ever-increasing number of chocolate chip cookies that my mom had left out to cool. The monster (I think people forget he is a monster by definition) kept finding loopholes in our deals, and the tension was getting higher and higher as the water rose in the creek. Cookie Monster smelled like BO and his eyes rolled around like a crazy person's. He was unstable. In the end, Daisy came through, as she always did.

Mom would start these stories, "When you were both very small, we had a wonderful dog named Daisy," and they quickly took on a life of their own. They eventually made their way into our collective consciousness as real events, complete with details not included in the original stories which must have been added by Sarah and me. It was years later, during some holiday involving drinking (see "every holiday"), that we started reminiscing about childhood memories and one of us asked: "Did we really have a dog when we were little? I kind of feel like we did, but I also can't picture us having a dog with all of the other animals we had. Daisy, maybe?" It wasn't until then that we realized these were, in fact, fictitious stories our mom had made up to keep us entertained on rainy days in our old house. Stories that drew on real events (being terrorized by a neighbor's dog, getting stuck in a creek, finding snakes, spiders, and arrowheads, etc.), with Daisy taking the place of our mother as the heroine.

I guess what I mean by this is, all of the stories in this book are exactly how I remember them, but I honestly remember having a flying southern-belle dog and interacting with Muppets. Take that how you want. I had a great childhood.

Oh, also – All views expressed are my own and do not reflect those of National Geographic, the National Geographic Channel, Icon Films, John Hunt Publishing, or any other person or organization mentioned (or not mentioned) in this book.

Introduction

Some of you may know me as the "(almost) King of the Jungle", "Legend Hunter", "that animal guy", "Beast Hunter" or "that guy who had cancer and catches snakes". Probably not, though. Despite having a couple dozen hours of international TV series to my name, and giving hundreds of talks and presentations, I don't really get recognized very often, unless we're talking about college kids in Guwahati, India, middle-aged men in the US, or preteen Indonesian girls – my key demographics it turns out. I struggle to name anything those groups have in common besides me.

I left my home in Upstate New York at 16 to live in a barn in southern Maine for a marine biology internship, and I haven't stopped exploring since. My passion for wildlife led me to create my own YouTube-based wildlife series in 2004 and has landed me spots on Animal Planet, Nat Geo, Nat Geo Wild, Travel Channel, SyFy, BBC and more. Half of the TV shows I've made have never seen the light of day, but they were all an adventure and there isn't a single one I wouldn't do again if given the chance. Besides TV, I work full time in biotech, which is its own sort of adventure – albeit one where drinking the water is generally safer. I've been bitten and stung by just about everything you can think of – from rattlesnakes and black bears to bullet ants and a rabid raccoon – and I've lost count of the number of countries I've been to.

I've had the opportunity to travel the world, interacting with some of the strangest and rarest animals, while having the honor of living with indigenous peoples in some of the most remote locations – participating in their rituals, eating traditional meals, and massively embarrassing myself while always trying to remain respectful. I am a perpetual fish out of water, even in my home state of Massachusetts. This book is part of the "On the Hunt" series, in which I get to tell some of my favorite stories from those travels.

My first TV series *Beast Hunter* did not just happen by chance, and this book is partially about how it came to be, partially how I started doing this in general, and partially what happens when you lose your dream job. In my case, you get cancer. I'm assuming that's not the same for everyone, but yeah – this book is also about cancer. Lots of cancer. And it's all rolled up in this messy, ridiculous, curse-filled package. But I'm getting ahead of myself. Let's start with me lying in a pit of 200,000 snakes, because that always seems like a good place to start.

Chapter 1

Snakes! Why'd It Have to be Snakes?

If you happen to find yourself, as I have, in a rock pit filled three-feet deep with approximately 200,000 live snakes, the first thing you'll notice is the smell. It's not a good smell, but not entirely nauseating either. It's more of an omnipresent unpleasantness, like the knowledge that certain politicians exist and certain close friends and family members definitely vote for them, no matter what they say at parties. It's there, always lingering, but never addressed. This odor, in the pit of snakes, is distinctly reptile and all-consuming, as if there were a reptilian world and that was the only reality you will ever know. "Oh, this is where I live now," you'll think. "This kind of sucks." It's not, "Holy shit my eyes are burning and at the same time I want to vomit," like, say, the scent of a litter box that hasn't been changed in a very long time, and all of the litter has hardened into one solid clump, with more litter dumped on top of that piss-brick until it hardens, and the cycle repeats itself until the entire eight inch tall litter box is a solid cake of cat urine and feces hardened into a cement-like slurry that even getting close to makes you feel like you are bathing in pure ammonia. No, it isn't that. I've experienced that, and it was a worse smell than 200,000 snakes. But the smell of 200,000 snakes is bad, man. It's really, really bad.

The next thing is the sound. You would've heard it from nearly a mile away as you approached the pit. It has a certain Lovecraftian other-ness. From a distance, it makes your skin crawl, just a little – something primal in the reptilian part of your brain tells you to turn around and head back, but you don't, and it gets louder and louder, until you are right on top of it. Then you go into the pit and, while the snakes are slithering through your hair, across the little bit of exposed skin above your beltline where your shirt has come untucked, and prying, face first, into your boots, it's shockingly loud. It's a rushing – like a wild, fast-flowing river. Not rapids, not broken by crashing into rocks – just a *whoooooooooooosh* of movement, an unyielding rustling of leaves. You need to speak up to be heard over it. It's the sound of millions of tiny reptile scales moving over rocks, leaves, sticks, you, and other reptiles.

The sight is beyond comprehension. We, humans, don't do well dealing with a swarm. We can't really process the sheer number of nonhuman creatures. Make the creatures snakes and it's the stuff of primeval nightmares. The physical manifestation of an ancestral concept of evil. An animal so entangled in so many Freudian dreams, so many iconographic concepts, so many deepest, darkest fears, and it's too much. I *love* snakes, and it was a lot to process. I've spent much of my life searching for snakes, finding one or two, and considering that a great day. Being confronted by hundreds of thousands of them – slithering, weighing down the branches of trees until the branch touches the ground, piles of them literally rolling down hills on top of a base-layer of snakes covering the ground. It was beautiful, and repulsive. It was Giger or Hirst – just madness, right in front of you.

The feeling is where most people would tap out. Most, but not Adolfo from the *Toucher and Rich* radio show, who described the feeling of the 16 foot python I put on his hefty, shirtless torso as "oddly arousing", much to the delight of the radio audience, and the massive discomfort of my wife. It's hard to describe the feeling of a snake to someone, much less hundreds of thousands of snakes. First off, they are not slimy, but also not rough – they feel a bit like well-cared-for leather. But it's the musculature underneath that's really unique. A snake's body is basically solid muscle covered by a sheath of interlocked, smooth scales. They are surprisingly heavy and firm. That's ONE snake. The feeling of 200,000? It's so overwhelming that you forget how strange it is. Holding one snake takes up a lot of your attention, holding a few leaves you feeling overwhelmed and unsure of where to put your hands, how to move, etc. Being several feet deep in a living carpet of snakes is so bonkers that it doesn't seem like real life. I started reaching into the mass of them and scooping them up, two-handed, then letting the piles cascade down my arms and body to rejoin the horde. Remember being in a ball pit at Chuck E. Cheese? You couldn't feel every ball any more than you could feel every strain of flu living on some of the balls, or each particle of vomit and urine on the others. They were just all around you, pressing against you, occasionally hitting you on the head or going down your pants. Same thing here, but, you know – snakes.

But, much stronger than all of these sensations, and much less anticipated, was a sudden and overwhelming existential crisis. Could I keep doing this? What was my goal in all of this absurdity? Why did I want to be a nature show host? Why do I put myself and my friends through this? What was wrong with me that this was how I had chosen to spend my birthday weekend the year after chemo, after putting my loved ones through hell? One year into the sentence I had been given – a 50% chance at being alive in five years? This was what I was going to do with my life? This was my bucket-list item – the thing I had most wanted to do? What was wrong with me? I was not having a "how did I get here?" moment as that part was crystal clear. But I did feel an incredible sense of guilt for enjoying this as much as I did, and the answer to the pervasive "where do I go from here?" was anything but clear.

Chapter 2

How Did I Get Here? Oh Yeah, That's Right – Cancer

I had cancer for around seven years before it was diagnosed. That messes with your head. I still get completely lost thinking about what that means 10 years after my diagnosis. That's seven years of my life when I had a biological time-bomb growing inside of me. Seven years of happy, carefree memories, when in reality I had a tumor slowly eating me from the inside. A small clump of my cells that decided, "Nah, fuck it, I'm not going to play by the rules." (Yes, I imagine my tumor as a bad cop from an eighties movie – mustache, aviators, you get the gist. My tumor's getting too old for this shit.) Its existence doesn't negate those memories, but it does cast a shadow over them.

It started growing right around the time I filmed the first TV series I was in – a reality show on *Animal Planet*. It means that the first apartment my wife Anna and I got together, the first time we traveled internationally together, the entire time I filmed my web series *Nature Calls*, my 30th birthday – I had cancer during all of it, and I didn't know it. My brain then makes the jump to the dark place, the "How do you know you don't have cancer now, Pat? Hm? You didn't know it then, you felt totally fine, how do you know the cancer's gone?" place. And, in truth, I don't know. I have learned to live with that voice, or at least not allow it to make me curl up in a ball on the couch and get lost in it. But, honestly – seven years before a diagnosis!

There were signs, I guess, but they were subtle. I did get frequent stomachaches, I had diarrhea more than most people, I think – although most people don't talk about how frequently they get diarrhea, and when I ask them they tell me I'm being "weird". Also, I once lost 21 pounds in a weekend. People don't believe me when I say that, but Anna can verify, she saw the before and after scale and encouraged me to go to a doctor, but I said, "I was heavy as a kid, I lose and gain weight really easily."

"Um, not 21 pounds, Pat, that is insane. That's like, 'published in a medical journal' weird."

"Nah, some of it was water weight, I'm sure." I completely wrote it off because I did gain and lose weight easily. Twenty-one pounds was extreme – but 10 pounds in a week I thought was normal. I didn't think about it much at the time, but that was probably the only red flag I might have picked up on. That was until I went into labor in Sumatra filming the fourth episode of the TV series *Beast Hunter* for Nat Geo and Icon Films.

I was a weird and awkward kid which should not be a surprise to anyone, as I am a weird and awkward adult. I started talking and walking at around six months old, and apparently my muscles weren't ready for either activity because I ended up with dislocating joints and a terrible speech impediment. No one other than my sister could understand most of what I said before I was four. She would translate, and sometimes the translation just happened to work out in her favor. "He's asking if we can have strawberry shortcake" (Sarah's favorite). She really could understand me though, and was the only person I could have an actual conversation with for a few years. I was in speech therapy from the age of three to six, and eventually, my mom's cousin, a speech therapist, got through to me and helped me make the right sounds at the right time – but my brain always worked faster than my tongue, and even once I'd gotten the sounds right my sentences were often jumbled, rambling, and slightly incomprehensible. Also, I'd be falling down all the time because none of my joints connected quite right, and my knees, hips, feet, shoulders, elbows, etc. would pop-out at inopportune times.

I've always struggled with anxiety as well. Whether it's innate or the product of being raised Roman Catholic is a hot topic of debate in my family, but part of it is being a fidgeter. I bite my nails, crack my knuckles, scratch my face stubble, and all that – but I also dislocate my joints. I just sit there, popping my shoulder in and out, in and out… It's made for fun party tricks over the years, and putting one leg over my head while standing has actually come in handy during a couple of job interviews, but, as a kid, these things don't really make a lot of other kids jump at the opportunity to be your friend. My innate love and encyclopedic knowledge of wildlife, coupled with the tendency to bring every conversation around to this subject, didn't help. Nor did my tendency to overeat and my willful ignorance of almost anything that other kids my age liked: TV, video games, sports, music, pop culture, movies – anything that helps most kids relate to each other wasn't really a part of my world.

I actually liked some of those things, just not the same ones the kids in my class did. I loved movies, but mainly musicals. I still do: *Bye Bye Birdie*, *West Side Story*, *On Moonlight Bay* – these were not the movies that boys my age talked about. My mom is a film buff and introduced my sister Sarah, four years my senior, and I to her favorites, and we both really took to it. We would act them all out and put on shows for the adults, Sarah doing choreography and me playing whatever role I was assigned. This led to other quirky film choices and questionable judgment calls by our parents – like letting a six-year-old watch *Little Shop of Horrors*, or a 10-year-old watch *Cry-Baby* and other John Waters movies. "We made you leave the room during any sex scenes," is all my mom says to defend herself. I don't think any defense is needed – they're great films and I'm glad we watched them, together, as a family – a weird, weird, loving, awesome, weird family.

For TV, I liked old cartoons and BBC wildlife documentaries almost exclusively. When I was out of school sick, my parents would let me rent any VHS I wanted, and without fail I would rent one of the *Life on Earth* tapes. For music I liked fifties and sixties pop, Weird Al, Dr. Demento, and, starting in 5th grade, punk and ska thanks to Sarah and her friends. In the eighties and early nineties, my parents were in a fifties cover band called The DeSotos, so dressing like a greaser with a pack of candy cigarettes rolled in the sleeve of my white T-shirt and my curly hair done in a "Duck's Ass" style (as my mom called it) seemed completely normal at eight years old. As did creating a dance routine to *Leader of the Pack* and *He's a Rebel* with Sarah. When I was wearing all mismatched plaid and homemade punk shirts in 7th grade, the kids in my class were, understandably, unable to really process what was happening. And I was always – and I mean always – obsessed with animals.

My mom will regularly tell a story about me filling a mayonnaise jar so full of bees that the bees could barely move while I was still in diapers. I stopped wearing diapers on my 2nd birthday and didn't have a single accident until I was 10 years old, when I became so focused on catching a squirrel that I forgot to pee until I finally caught it, then peed my pants. As a parent now, this bee-catching story boggles my mind. The pant wetting at 10 raises questions I'd rather not explore. But the bees – how did that happen? I don't for a second doubt it's true. I can remember doing it, in fact. I can remember events from before I turned one – not stories about them, but the actual events. Not a lot, but I have real memories from being eight or nine months old. So, I'm not yet two years old, and my mom, who is allergic to bees, sends me outside with a glass jar and watches from the kitchen window while I slam the jar down on the ground again and again sliding the lid back to slam it down, then bringing the lid underneath to pick it up again. She thought I was catching ladybugs as this was a hobby of mine, until I came back into the house proudly carrying a buzzing jar filled with dozens of angry honeybees.

While the neighborhood kids played ball, I can remember

spending hours sitting on these huge bulkhead doors leading to our basement watching this hairy, metallic-green spider catch and eat small bugs. I didn't want bedtime stories from my mom, I wanted wildlife encyclopedias. She would take my sister, my best friend Adam and me to the library, and I would come home with a stack of wildlife guides and then ask her to read them to me, which she did without complaint. Not stories – just facts about animals. Then I'd ask her for clarifications: "What does crepuscular mean? What is parthenogenesis? How does bioluminescence work?" You know, normal kid questions. When I was four and Sarah was eight, Sarah had a friend over to play. While we were all sitting around and eating dinner I suddenly looked up and asked, "Do people mate like hippos?" We'd watched an Attenborough hippo special earlier in the week, and I couldn't stop thinking about how cool they were. My father without missing a beat replied, "Pretty much, yeah, but not usually in the water." My mortified sister almost started crying.

My room, our basement, and our yard were always filled with various containers which were filled with various creatures. My mom was always my biggest supporter, and did everything to help me care for my growing menagerie. She would wake up at 5am to start chopping up worms to feed to baby birds, help track down the right leaves for the various caterpillars (which required acquiring a working knowledge of botany and another array of field guides), or fill gallon jugs every afternoon with fresh water from the creek for my crayfish and pollywogs. She was, and is, the best Mom I could have possibly asked for, and a huge reason why I became the person I am.

She drew the line at rodents, though. She has a phobia of small and furry creatures. I could keep wolf spiders, mantises, snakes – anything except rodents. So I hid those from her in shoeboxes and old containers in the woods, under the porch, and other places where she wouldn't go. I bred poisonous spiders when I was five and kept a cottonmouth in our basement when

I was seven. I told her it was a "wood snake", and she said she didn't remember reading about any "wood snake" and seemed a little suspicious, but we had *a lot* going on in our house at the time – it was summer, so there were frog's eggs hatching, fish that needed their water changing, birds coming and going, cats that needed flea treatments, and my sister, myself, and the other kids who were always around, so she forgot about the "wood snake" for a few days.

Then one Saturday morning I heard a scream from the basement. "PATRICK! PATRICK! GET YOUR BUTT DOWN HERE, TOUT-SUITE, NOW, MISTER! THIS SNAKE HAS A THICK ARROW-SHAPED HEAD! Did you bring a venomous snake into our house?"

Uh-oh. "Um, well, I was really excited and I wanted to milk it because I've read a lot about how to do that, but never done it, and I thought I could, but I wanted to feed him first, but I can't figure out what he eats because I think he's a cottonmouth, but maybe he's a copperhead, and cottonmouths don't live around here, so it would be really interesting if he is, and I've been trying to figure it out, can you help me please?"

She did help me – after she calmed down, and patiently (far more patiently than I deserved) explained that the *new* rule was no rodents, *and* nothing venomous.

She brought me to meet one of my heroes, a local wildlife presenter named Dean Davis who confirmed that it was a cottonmouth, and talked to me all about how unique it was to find one a couple hundred miles north of their known range. My parents regularly drove me hours to see Dean's shows, and having a real conversation with him about snakes was tantamount to being called into the dugout to strategize plays with the first-base coach of the Red Sox (fill in your preferred sports analogy here – I don't know anything about sports so I hope that worked). It was a big deal for me.

While I loved herps and bugs, my true passion was always

and still is marine life. As a kid I was over-the-top obsessed with the ocean and everything in it. The first time I remember seeing the ocean was when I was three. I remember getting to Seabrook Beach with a metal Folgers coffee can in one hand and a butterfly net in the other, and just stopping dead in my tracks, unable to move, transfixed by the immensity of the Atlantic Ocean in front of me. The mysteries it must contain, the creatures hidden in it, the fact that I was going to get in the same water that some of weirdest animals I'd read about lived in. It was more than my developing brain could take, and I just couldn't move. My parents laughed and carried me like a statue to the spot we were going to claim for the day. My mom slathered sunblock on me, changed me, and forced a Capri-Sun down my throat before I was able to move and speak. "Mom, that's the ocean. We're at the ocean. That's where giant squid live, and nautilus, and anglerfish." Because of my speech impediment, what they heard was, "Mawm, dats da o-sin. Weiw at da o-sin. Dats weiw giant squid wiv an nautiwus an angwah fiss." I had to be physically pulled away from the water and tidepools and forced to eat that day. From that moment, the ocean was my life.

I was pulled between the worlds of herps and marine. I remember explaining this to my 3rd grade teacher, who genuinely encouraged my scientific curiosity by helping me spell "Either Marine Biologist or Herpetologist" on my "What I want to be when I grow up" report, and allowing me to leave the classroom, alone, and go into the field near the school to catch animals we could raise in the back of the class. In third grade. When I was 8. "Well, Patrick finishes his assignments hours before the other kids, and it's either that or let him stare out the window," is what she told my not-at-all concerned parents, who thought it was wonderful that I'd caught the class a few frogs, a toad, a newt, a salamander, and a garter snake. The eighties were a different time.

I grew up in Wynantskill, New York, a town just outside of

Troy close to Albany, which is inexplicably the capital of the state that also contains New York City. My favorite facts about Wynantskill are:

1. The entire town was a potato farm in the 1600s, and while exploring the woods we would occasionally find wild potatoes still growing in the hills.
2. Everyone called the river in town a "crick" and the local church fair a "bazaar", and no one thought it was weird.
3. In 1994 the only burger joint in town, which opened in 1938, added cheese to its menu and it was a front-page story in the newspaper and all anyone talked about that summer at the bazaar.

It was incredible being a kid in Wynantskill. Adam and I spent every day in the spring, summer, and fall exploring the woods, fishing in the crick, swimming anywhere the water was deeper than two feet, catching frogs, salamanders, snakes, and bugs, squirt-gun fights that lasted all day, picking wild blackberries and strawberries and bringing them to my mom or grandmother to bake with, pricking our fingers in the process and becoming "blood brothers" with each other and our other friends Andrew and Katie-Rose, climbing through drainpipes, falling in the various cricks, streams, ponds, and lakes, riding bikes until dark, letting ourselves into any neighbors' house to use the bathroom or get a glass of water – it really genuinely was like we somehow took the best parts of the 1950s and preserved them in that place. Winters were for entire neighborhood-sized snowball fights, gathering the "daredevil club" for sledding down my back hill (which we called the mudslide), walking over frozen and semi-frozen streams, and reading about wildlife.

Growing up in Wynantskill didn't offer much in the way of marine life, though, so by third grade I'd figured out a way to bring it to me. Our annual week in Seabrook was a salve to fill this void in my life. Every year, we would get two souvenirs: a theme T-shirt (Miami Mice, Not Playing With a Full Duck, Ghostbusters, etc.) from the Hampton Boardwalk, and something under $5. I would scour the beach collecting shells, sand dollars, and urchin shells, and convince my parents that if we left them out in the sun all week they wouldn't smell by the time we left, and I could take them home (spoiler alert – they always smell), but found I could use my under-$5 souvenir allowance to add to this collection and get a dried seahorse, pipefish, blowfish, or other sea creature. One year, Sarah saw how much I wanted a huge pufferfish and gave up her souvenir so I could go up to $10 on it. By the time I was 12, every surface of my room was covered in either an aquarium, a mayo jar filled with something alive, or a dead sea creature. I'd also taken the more prized specimens and hung them from a fishing line duct taped or stapled to my ceiling, making my room feel like you were under the sea! Really, it was probably closer to being in the movie *Seven* when they discover "Sloth" in the room filled with air fresheners hanging from the ceiling – mine not so much masking the scent of decay and death as creating it.

Sarah was my hero and protector when I was growing up. We are almost nothing alike, but are very definitely from the same family – you can hear it in the way we talk and our mannerisms. She was always popular, cool, and surrounded by a vast array of friends, while I always had a small group of close friends, was nerdy before it was cool to be nerdy, and was surrounded by bugs and reptiles. Sarah's social status at school helped keep me safe from the worst bullies – when an older football player is trying to date your sister, the other guys in the school tend to cut you more slack. She also went out of her way to make sure no one messed with her little brother. She once marched into my first-grade classroom in the middle of a lesson and picked up a kid who had been bullying me (he peed on my shoes in the bathroom and punched me in the face), and yelled at him in front of the class, then apologized to the teacher and walked out. She knew I was a weirdo, but no one else better say it.

My room was a testament to that weirdness, and I loved it. It was my happy place filled with live and dead animals and a rainbow painted on the wall by my Aunt Nancy. I also had animal posters everywhere, but not cute animals – think less kittens and more scientific charts, marine life size comparisons, and evolutionary trees. I eventually moved onto real marine biology, and when I left home at 16 and lived on my own for the first time, it was for a marine bio internship in Maine. A friend asked what the nightlife was like in southern Maine. I replied, with no hesitation or sense of irony: "Great! It's really awesome! There are foxes, raccoons, lightning bugs, polyphemus moths, and so far I've spotted two species of owls!"

I lived in a barn, by myself, willingly, in order to do marine bio research when I was 16 and 17. I learned a lot that year – how to cook after forgetting to eat for an entire day and desperately opening a can of beef stew with pliers and eating it cold, doing laundry after wearing clothes until they smelled so bad I was offensive to be around, and how to be okay with being alone. The barn was never locked, and occasionally a 21-year-old woman (whom I of course had a crush on, and no, of course nothing happened with because she wasn't a creep) would stay there, teach me life skills, and drive me places, while random groups of bird researchers would stay a night or two and leave dead specimens in the fridge. For the most part though it was just me and my thoughts.

I grew up a lot. I learned that adults were trying to figure things out as they went along, the same as kids. I had my first real taste of freedom and was never able to fully live at home again. I also discovered the first barracuda ever caught in Maine and named it "Eva", which the newspaper took to be a clever play on Eve, as in the first woman, but really it was because it was the "first one eva". (I was 16, don't judge me.) I gave a lot of marine biology talks that year, and learned that I enjoyed wildlife education. I had been doing it my whole life, but thought maybe I'd want to formalize it in some way. I always had a crowd gathered around me to see what animal I had just caught and to hear all about it, but in Maine that crowd was organized, and I liked getting people as enthused about wildlife as me – generally through a high tolerance for pain and lots of self-deprecating humor. One of the best things about working with animals in front of the public is that if I don't get bitten, everyone assumes I really know what I'm doing. But if I DO get bitten, everyone is super excited and thinks I'm really bad ass. It's win-win, except for the effects of the bites. It's a good thing I don't mind scars.

I moved to Boston to go to Suffolk University. I majored in marine biology and applied that love of public speaking to teaching labs and field classes. I drove a huge van filled with college freshman up to northern Maine to assist on a marine biology fieldtrip almost every year from 1998 to 2012 and I loved it. When I graduated though, I realized that "biologist street performer" wasn't a thing, or at least anything that paid, and I had student loans, so I got a job in biotech and promptly helped one of my best friends and former roommate Adrianna get hired as well. She and I shared a desk for six years, after being roommates our freshman year and taking every class together for all four years, and I kept giving impromptu talks while on hikes or day trips to the beach. I also made a conscious decision to stay in Boston. I loved my adopted hometown.

Eventually, Anna, my girlfriend who I am now married to, told me I was worrying parents when I'd hold up a horseshoe crab and teach the gathered crowd of kids about it, and I should somehow get some credibility so they know I was not some creep trying to lure their kids away, just some weird adult who really, really likes wild animals and public speaking. Weird, but harmless. Maybe I should do TV like I'd always said I wanted to.

She saw an ad on Animal Planet looking for the "next wildlife host" via a reality competition show called *King of the Jungle 2*, so we made an audition tape. It was really bad and I knew it, so, after talking to Anna and Adrianna, I told the micro lab I was working at that I needed a few days off and the next morning drove 14 hours, in the snow, to the nearest open audition, at the Columbus Zoo in Ohio.

My car broke down once on the way there – coincidentally and conveniently very close to my parents' house in Upstate NY. After a minor repair, I was back on the road having officially maxed out my first credit card. I didn't think I'd be able to afford a hotel in Ohio and thought I could find a spot to sleep in my car before the audition but one of my best friends, Joe, had a better idea. He had a good friend whom I had never met, BK, who graciously agreed to let me crash in his apartment in Columbus. He wasn't going to be there when I arrived but left the keys for me – a stranger – based on Joe's vouching for me. In return, I left him a two six-packs. I slept on BK's couch that night in his empty apartment and was the first in line at 4am the next day.

In my audition I put one leg behind my head while standing and telling a ridiculous story about the time I was attacked by a rabid racoon on a marine bio internship in Maryland. I then told the casting director, as I was putting my second leg behind my head, that everyone *thinks* they want to see you put both legs behind your head, until you actually do it. I wasn't wrong, but they asked me to come back the next day for the second round of auditions. I stayed the night at the condo of two veterinarians I had met in line waiting to audition. The next day I talked about my time as the bassist and growling-vocalist in the punk band "Plan 10" (so named because in Ed Woods' classic film, "Plan 9" failed), working for The Mighty Mighty Bosstones, and spouted off some random animal facts while playing with an armadillo they provided. "These are so cool! They actually carry leprosy! I've always wanted to catch one – not leprosy, but an armadillo!

Some species can inflate their guts to float!" Etc.

I ended up getting picked to be on the show, finishing in 2nd place, and realized that I really liked making TV. I'd made friends with the crew through the course of filming KOTJ2, and asked the Animal Planet folks what I needed to do to get a show. They said they'd like to see footage of me as a host, as opposed to a contestant, but didn't want to sponsor any filming, so I made my own nature show.

I put flyers up all over Boston to find a cameraperson, roped Anna and a couple of friends into helping, and created *Nature Calls* – a web-based punk-rock wildlife adventure series that I wrote, produced, edited, starred in, directed, and paid for. It would suck up all of my free time and available credit for six years. Creating *Nature Calls* was the fun part – the trips to Costa Rica, Arizona, etc. Even the late nights of learning how to edit and mix audio were fun, but I was also making regular trips to Washington DC, NYC, and occasionally CA and Colorado to meet with production companies and networks and pitch *Nature Calls* and other wildlife-adventure series ideas. This meant sleeping on buses, planes, and family members', friends', and friends-of-friends' couches in all of these cities and financing it all myself on an ever-growing roster of maxed out credit cards. I was working 60+ hour weeks at my biotech job and putting in at least another 40 into *Nature Calls* for most of those six years – my record was 21 days in a row at the lab, with none being less than 10 hour shifts, and one 19 hours, while at the same time editing a teaser reel that a network had asked for, setting up a meeting with Nickelodeon and writing three series pitches. Besides horrific sleep health, *Nature Calls* also brought me two of my best friends, some of my favorite travel memories, and eventually a few pilots, appearances, and my own TV series.

Beast Hunter started with a phone call from the CEO of Icon Films, Harry Marshall. Harry had been a hero of mine since I caught some footage he had filmed of tigers, which normally did nothing for me. I've always been more of a reptile guy, but Harry made tigers exciting. This doesn't sound like a hard thing to do – I mean, they're *tigers* after all – but believe me they have never been shown, before or since, in the way that Harry presented them. They appeared as almost spiritual beings in the footage, and their story was the story of India, a land the filmmaker clearly loved. Their interactions with the world around them become almost operatic when presented by Harry. Their personalities were displayed without any Disneyfication – they were able to be tigers, but amazing, complex, interesting tigers rather than the easy, "Hey aren't these big cats terrifying *and* cute AT THE SAME TIME?" tigers. So getting a phone call from this man, whom I'd admired for so long, left me speechless – not a great trait during what turned out to be a job interview. Harry e-mailed first and asked for a call. I agreed immediately, but was terrified he was going to ask me what my experience was with tigers, cobras, or freshwater fish as his biggest series to date had been with these groups. Luckily, he was looking for something different – very different.

Harry mentioned he had seen a lot of my work – *Nature Calls*, some pilots I had filmed for Animal Planet, and random other clips. He went on to say he really enjoyed them, mentioning he had a project going with National Geographic, and asked if I might be interested. I said of course I was. There was no one on Earth I would have rather worked for than Harry, and no organization than Nat Geo. I wouldn't have cared if his next words were, "We want to make a series about men who dress as female hippos and get males to mate with them. We'll provide the SCUBA training." I would have said, "I'm the perfect guy to do that!" with no hesitation. Luckily, this was not what Harry had in mind – I definitely would have died filming that series. He wanted to do a show exploring persistent myths around the world and their cultural importance to indigenous people, and asked what I knew about Cryptozoology, a notoriously fuzzy scientific discipline, which he was hoping I could bring some credibility to.

Fortunately, it was a subject I was well versed in. I had never grown out of the sense of scientific wonder about what could possibly be lurking in the dark places of the world. Most kids get a book on Bigfoot or the Loch Ness Monster and call it a day – as a budding biologist, I read Darwin, Dawkins, and Quammen, but also Coleman, Heuvelman, and Dinsdale. I loved the possibilities and found my scientific self constantly arguing with my cryptozoologist self, no side ever winning.

After giving my thoughts on a few cryptids, Harry asked if I had ever heard of a man named Charles Fort. I replied, "That's my great-uncle!" This was followed by complete silence on the line. After a moment, I said, "Harry? Hello? Did I lose you?" The very British Harry apologized for the silence and simply said, "No shit?", a very non-British response.

I explained that I had grown up being told by my Grandmother, Hattie, that "You're just like your uncle Charlie," but I never knew who this mysterious "uncle Charlie" was. I didn't think that he was a direct relation, since I had never seen him at any of the Spain BBQs, so I thought that maybe he was an "Uncle" like other friends of my Grandparents whom I was asked to call "Uncle." My favorite of these pretend relations was a guy who lived in the Philippians and brought wooden toys and told great stories about exotic wildlife whenever he visited — maybe Charlie was like this, and I'd meet him one day. All I knew about him was that whenever Hattie saw me catching, reading about, or discussing weird animals — the comparison to uncle Charlie would be uttered.

It wasn't until I was a teenager when Hattie asked what I was reading and I mentioned "The Book of the Damned" that she said, excitedly, "By Charles Fort? That's your uncle Charlie!" and proceeded to show me her collection of his books, signed and dedicated to various family members. I don't know who was more shocked, me, or Harry when this connection came to light.

Harry was excited, I was excited – we laughed and started planning the series right then, bouncing ideas off each other, tweaks, suggestions, and potential episodes. It was the start of what I consider my most important collaborative relationship other than my wife. Every time I talk to Harry I feel like we can accomplish anything, and the ideas we start with at the beginning of a conversation are tenfold better by the end of it.

Beast Hunter, then called *Wild Thing*, was born. I would travel the world, live with various tribes and peoples – participating in their rituals, eating their food, learning from them, etc. – and take a scientific approach to some classic myths. I'd propose mistaken identity while showcasing the known creatures of the area, look at the cultural and historic importance of the legend, and give my honest opinion on the likelihood of the stories, never actually seeking to prove or disprove the animal's existence. My mind would be changed, a number of times, and I would come to believe that, outrageous as it seemed, some of these animals actually are out there. I wanted to quit my microbiology biotech job that day and start, but it would be another 10 months of meetings, trips to DC, writing and rewriting, filming test clips, contract negotiations, and conversations with my day job before I was actually on a plane and on my way to film the first episode for Nat Geo. At the time of writing it's more than 10 years later, and I still work in biotech. Lesson number one in going for your dream job – don't quit your day job.

So, back to being in labor – fourth episode, tons of travel, insane schedules, etc. I woke up one morning in Sumatra feeling distinctly unwell, but chalked it up to the amount of bizarre foods I'd been consuming and the three hours of sleep a night I'd been getting due to the insane filming schedule. It was 2010 – about six months before my diagnosis – and we'd been in Sumatra for a week filming the 4th episode of *Beast Hunter*. A few hours after waking up, I discovered the meaning of the term "violently ill". I found myself writhing on the ground in stomach-churning agony with the worst gastrointestinal pain I had experienced up to that point in my life. I was vomiting from the pain, nearly blacking out, and contorting my body while lying on pillows that the crew had placed on a dais in a restaurant's back garden. This description, "dais in the back garden", conveys more of a sense of beauty than is deserved. Being a raised platform it was technically a "dais", but based on its upkeep it would have fit better in a horror movie than a relaxing meditation retreat, and I appeared not to be the first person to vomit on it. And yes, given that it was a garden behind the restaurant, it was a "back garden", but again, horror movie houses have backyards too. I don't want to belabor the point, I just don't want you imaging a picturesque, serene, southeast Asian paradise. This was more a backlot that smelled of cigarettes and diesel, was oppressively hot and humid, with the sounds of traffic filling the air intermingled with my grunts of pain and the meows of kittens with missing limbs and ribs showing from hunger.

The waves of pain would come every 10 minutes and last for about two. In the remaining time I would catch my breath and assure the wait staff that a massage would definitely not make me feel any better, but thank you for offering. There was a suggestion I should go to a hospital, but our fixer (the person who translates, gets you from place to place, keeps you alive and out of trouble, etc.), a British man who had lived in Sumatra for years, strongly advised against it, saying: "Mate, I'd rather deal with whatever you've got than what they might give you." So the pain kept coming. Gradually, the intervals between the pain increased and the pain of the episodes decreased to the point where it only felt like bad cramps every hour or so. I was offered more massages (to this day I don't know what was up with that), given a lot of Pocari Sweat drink (the first ingredient is air!), and then – well, we had a lot of filming to do and had lost an entire morning, so we got back to work. The day before that incident was the last time in my life that I felt "100% good". The following month was particularly nasty, with this scenario repeating itself a few times at random inconvenient moments.

The crew decided I must be pregnant and started referring to the incident as "when Pat was in labor". There were a lot of jokes about how surprised Anna would be when I got home. Would I name the baby after them? They thought I'd been putting on some weight but didn't want to say anything. Now it made sense why I was eating such bizarre foods. Could Pinkie, the orangutan who had violated me (long story), be the father? It's awesome having a crew of all guys around – such kindness and decency when facing illness.

Anna will get a lot of mentions from here on out, so it's best to introduce her properly. We met in 1999 at Suffolk University when she was a freshman and I was a sophomore. Despite looking more than 10 years younger than me, there's actually only nine months between us. I will never forget the first time I saw her, as it was the only time in my life I have been left literally speechless by a woman I've never spoken to. She was in a dress on her way out for the night, and I was in some dirty army pants and an old Ramones T-shirt hanging out in the cafeteria. I pretended to study the overhead menu for the entire duration she was in line and made awkward eye contact a few times, but was physically unable to speak. She was probably (rightfully) weirded out by me. She made her exit, I regained my ability to function, and I told my friends that the most attractive woman I'd ever seen had just walked out of the room.

I figured out who she was a few weeks later when it turned out that I'd be the Teaching Assistant in her intro to chem lab. I spent the next few years getting to know her – teaching a couple of her labs, assisting the teacher in others, hanging out occasionally as friends, selling her my old books. Any excuse to talk to her. I literally wrote things down to say to her the night before our labs together, then lost my nerve and just talked about the subject matter at hand, or her trip to Vietnam when she was 14 (my go-to "Hey, I know a fact about you!" bullshit discussion). I sat awkwardly on my lab stool flicking my gloves against my thumb to make them "pop" and stared off into space, because I'm super cool like that. I finally got the courage to ask her out on a date at the start of my senior year. She had transferred to a different university in Boston and we were both single, and to my amazement she said yes. Our first date was at the New England Aquarium – which is the most Pat Spain thing to do, ever – and it was closed – which is actually *the* most Pat Spain thing to do, ever. We then went to a nice Italian restaurant, and when I tried being classy and asked if we should order some wine she looked really nervous, and said, "Ummmm... I better not."

To which I replied: "Oh, I just thought wine might be nice. I'm not trying to get you drunk and take advantage of you or anything." Those words actually left my mouth.

She just said: "I mean, I'm only 20..." For those of you not in the States, the drinking age here is 21, and Anna was only trying to avoid an awkward situation of not being able to produce valid ID to get a drink, so of course, I created a *much* more awkward situation. She married me. I still don't know how or why.

Anna is 5'3" and fiercer and more loyal than anyone you could meet. She's first-generation Vietnamese and grew up in the city featured in the 1995 documentary film *High on Crack Street*, Lowell, Massachusetts, which, if she's been drinking, she will usually tell you in the form of a shouted, "I'm from LOWELL," and an implied, "Don't fuck with me or my family" – sometimes it's not "implied" so much as "implicitly stated". She's amazing in every way – an amazing mom, funny, kind, and supersmart (she destroyed me in organic and all other chem classes, overall Grade Point Average, and, you know, life). She would have been totally fine if I'd come home and told her I was pregnant – if that was physiologically possible.

After getting back to Boston, I started trying to figure out what these labor pains really were. I went to a highly recommended gastroenterologist who, over the course of six months, diagnosed me with everything from stress (truth) and anxiety (double truth) to gluten allergies (not so much – but we did have a disgusting "gluten-free Thanksgiving" that year thanks to that incorrect diagnosis) and "post-traumatic GI distress", which apparently is a thing when you've gotten a really bad stomach bug, and then your entire body is so freaked out by it that you have to eat "clean" for a few months to reset your system into not repeating the symptoms every time you eat anything that triggers an association with the illness. I was checked for parasites multiple times, given maybe a dozen different prescriptions, pooped in many receptacles at multiple different locations for analysis, had my butt swabbed and many more invasive "internal exams" on multiple occasions, with the end result being: "Well, we still aren't sure what's wrong."

I have a long list of medical mishaps and weirdnesses, including: multiple head staples, the "most impacted wisdom teeth" the orthodontist had ever seen, mono, strep, and tonsillitis at the same time (on New Year's Eve 1999 when I was designated driver for our group), getting a pencil eraser stuck in my ear when I was nine and the terrible infection resulting from it, trigger finger on my ring finger, the aforementioned ability to dislocate any of my joints at will, kidney stones, hernias, a torn uvula, and waking up during an appendectomy.

I had my appendix out when I was 18 and away at school in Boston. My father dropped me off after winter break and, as he was leaving, I mentioned I had a bit of a stomachache, but it was probably from all the Christmas fudge and meatballs I'd eaten that week. The next day I couldn't get out of bed because my stomach hurt so bad, and the day after that my roommate insisted on walking me to the school infirmary. Once there I was greeted by a doctor and a nurse. The doctor listened to my symptoms (intense stomach pain, lack of appetite, shooting pain in my right side) and gave me a handful of condoms. I said, "Thank you, but I don't think these will help." He said, "Maybe not NOW, but they will help, in the future," and gave me a wink and a nudge. The nurse gave an eyeroll and let out a sigh. The doctor then asked a lot of questions allegedly "about my physical and mental health", but there were a lot more sex-related questions than expected.

He did a series of tests, then the nurse repeated these tests and asked less sex-oriented questions, and more medically significant ones. They consulted in front of me, arguing a bit, then the doctor said, "Well, we think you have appendicitis and we should send you to the ER for surgery because it's been a few days, and that… well, isn't good" (I knew this, as my great-uncle had died from appendicitis). "But, just to be safe," he continued, putting on rubber gloves like in a bad comedy, "I think we should do a full rectal exam."

To which the nurse said: "What the fuck, Ed? Really? Why would you do that? There is no need for a rectal exam." Then, seeming to remember I was there, added: "Doctor."

"Well, as you know, we can rule out some potent –"

"No," she cut him off. "No, I don't want to hear it. You are not doing a rectal exam on this kid. C'mon, we're getting you in a cab."

I thought the exchange was weird, but so much happened over the course of the next few days that I didn't have too much time to think about it. They put me in a cab – not an ambulance, a Boston cab (the driver was pissed) – and sent me to a "teaching hospital" where the diagnosis of appendicitis was confirmed via ultrasound within about 20 minutes of arrival, but since it was a "teaching hospital" I was examined by no less than 10 med students over the course of a few hours "while the surgery was prepped", who were all told by the head doctor: "Imagine you *didn't* have the results of the ultrasound in front of you. How would *you* diagnose this patient?"

"Um, I would push on his stomach and…"

"Jim, don't tell *me*. The patient is right here – go ahead and do it."

"Oh, right," chuckled Jim, and turned to me. "Hello, sir, my name is Doctor Franklin and I'm going to perform an exam to determine what the issue is. Do I have permission to put my hands on you and conduct this exam?"

Me, confused as shit and in intense and ever-increasing pain, "WHAT IS HAPPENING?!?!"

"Hey, Pat, remember, this is a teac –"

"YES, fine, for the third time, Doctor, Jesus. This is just really hurting and it's hard to concentrate."

"Thank you, Mr. Spain. Yes, I see you're in a considerable amount of stress and –"

"Pain! Yes, this really hurts, when is the surgery?"

"Well, Pat, as Doctor Franklin has said here, we are trying to determine what's wrong. We [chuckling] can't just rush into a random surgery without a diagnosis [wink wink]."

"But, you said the ultrasound showed that I have acute appendicitis and need surgery, now. Like, right now."

"Well, yes, but right now we are *imagining* what we would do if we didn't have that amazing ultrasound. There are a lot of cases that are less cut and dr –"

"OH MY GOD FINE! Do whatever. Oh man, this hurts."

"Jim, please continue with Mr. Spain's exam."

"Okay, so, when I push on your stomach… here… does it hurt more when I push in like this? Or when I rel –"

"AHHHHHHHHH!! SHIT! FUCK! Yes, that hurt more. Wow, that's really weird [laugh-crying]. It didn't hurt too bad when you pushed in but when you let go, wow," I said, with shaky breath cry-laughing. "Wow."

"Okay, we're not going to do that again, but that's classic

appendicitis. Jaimie, what would you ask Mr. Spain?"

"Well, if he were a woman, I would ask about any issues with his menstrual cycle, but, since he doesn't have ovaries – you don't have ovaries do you, Mr. Spain?" I shook my head, utterly defeated. "Since he doesn't have ovaries, we can rule that out. I guess I would ask him to stand on one leg and hop up and down?"

"Don't tell *me*, tell *him*, Jaimie."

"Mr. Spain, could you stand up, stand on one leg, and hop?"

Oh my God. How did I get here? "Sure, I will hop on one leg now." I did so. "Huh, nothing happened."

"Other leg, please."

I stood on the other leg, hopped, and immediately crumpled to the ground, "Oh, Jesus Christ. WOW, OH MAN, I have to lay down. That really, really hurt."

"Classic appendicitis."

"Yes! Karen, what would *you* ask Mr. Spain?"

This went on for two hours until, as my appendix started to rupture, surgery was finally ready. I was given the good drugs, asked to count backwards from 20, and my sister, looking frazzled, burst into the room and gave me a hug before I reached 15 and blacked out. Sarah had started traveling from NYC right after the first call from the infirmary and had made it with seconds to spare. The next thing I remember after saying the word, "Sarah!" was waking up during surgery. Yup. I was suddenly fully conscious and feeling really weird. As soon as I could see things I yelled, "OWWWWW! That hurts! Holy shit! I really have to pee."

A very startled doctor said, "Oh no, you're not supposed to be awake, buddy," not inspiring confidence.

"No! I REALLY have to pee, bad."

"Umm, don't worry about that, pal. Help!" he said the last bit to someone else.

Then a mask was over my face, and I lost consciousness.

I forgot about the pervy doctor who had given me condoms for a couple of years, until I was telling the story to a group of friends during my junior year of college. When I reached the part about the nurse objecting to the rectal exam, one of my friends said, "NO WAY! I went to the infirmary with the flu and he did a rectal exam! I thought it was weird."

"The bald guy with a ponytail?" asked another friend. "I went there with strep throat and he told me a rectal exam would be the best way to 'rule anything else out'."

So, the moral of this story is – if your doctor suggests a rectal exam for anything non-butt related, get a second opinion.

With all of that in my history, these random bouts of stomach pain didn't seem that odd. I was still leaving the country to film in Brazil and the UK, recording voiceover, writing more episodes, promoting the show, and working my day job. None of the stomach episodes were as bad as the first, so I didn't think too much about it. I just wanted it to go away so I could watch *Harry Potter* in the theater in England without feeling like I was going to puke and poop myself.

Had it not been for *Beast Hunter* and all of the crazy travel, foods, rituals, and sleeping situations, I probably would have left it alone and hoped it would get better. I only pushed for a diagnosis because there were so many potential travel-related causes. Had I been exposed to parasites? You bet I had! I had gotten Loa-Loa worm in the Central African Republic (which makes your entire body itch as the millions of worms living in your body die and are expelled. If you are exposed to it multiple times, you can see adult worms crawl across your eyeball), bed bugs in Mongolia, ticks and leeches all over me in Sumatra, chicken mites in Brazil, and more mosquito and fly bites than I had thought possible over the past year. This wasn't something I wanted to walk away from! I knew there was a chance this was some bad shit, but cancer never crossed my mind.

Chapter 3

"Cancer? That's Not So Bad. It's Not Like 'Cancer' or Something... Wait."

After ruling out essentially everything else, my doctors were at a loss. I was a 30-year-old who ate healthy, exercised daily, didn't smoke, occasionally drank, and had periodic bouts of stomach pain. The doctor at one point actually said, "It could be nothing or it could be AIDS, it's really hard to rule anything in or out."

"Well, ruling out AIDS is easy, right? Since I took an AIDS test and it was negative."

"You know what I mean."

Doctors shouldn't say that, but I did know what he meant. It wasn't parasites, Crohn's, IBS, acid reflux, diverticulitis, or severe hemorrhoids. Just as I was starting to go down the route of looking for possible allergies, I noticed blood in my stool – not like from wiping too hard, but *in* my stool. That made the doctor take notice. He said, "I don't think it's absolutely necessary, but we can always do a colonoscopy and an endoscopy."

"Yes, let's do that," I said without really knowing what an endoscopy was, while having a pretty good idea what a colonoscopy was – the "scope" and "colon" gave it away.

"Are you sure? I really feel like we can look into allergies," said my doctor.

"Let's just do the colonoscopy and rule the big stuff out," I said, thereby becoming the first patient to talk his doctor into doing a colonoscopy.

"Okay, if you're sure."

The last thing I remember before the procedure was my doctor saying, "I *really* don't think this is necessary, but if it will make you feel better to rule out anything really serious, we'll do it."

Then, like the appendectomy before it, and despite telling them the waking-up story, I woke up during the procedure. It didn't hurt too bad, but I felt like there was something inside of me hitting a wall that it shouldn't hit. So, you know, not pleasant by any means. After a bit it really did hurt, and I started crying and tensed up.

"Please don't do that," asked an exasperated doctor.

"I can't help it, you have a camera and a drain-snake up my butt," I replied in a drug haze.

"Please give Mr. Spain more meds." Then everything the doctor was saying got jumbled and unclear, because of the drugs. I started hearing bits and pieces of what he was saying, "Please try to relax. Something that shouldn't be there. Mass. Relax. Not good. See on the screen? Blockage. Blood. Stop clenching, please. Mass. Not good..."

After the procedure, when I was fully awake, the now sweaty-looking doctor said, "Mr. Spain, Pat, I'm really terribly sorry. I was wrong."

"Yeah, that was not painless. In fact, that sucked. What happened?"

"That's not what I meant, but I'm sorry about that as well. Do you have a family member here? You are still on a lot of medication and I need to explain the situation to someone."

As a heads up, when a doctor "needs to explain a situation" to someone who is not on a lot of meds, it's usually not good. I didn't think that at the time though – at the time, I was just enjoying the drugs and not having something up my butt.

"My girlfriend, yeah, you can tell her."

The doctor left to get Anna, who came in and sat next to me, while I hummed and swung my legs while sitting on the doctor's table. "Hi! That was not fun. The doctor wants to talk to us, why do you look worried?"

The doctor took out a series of printouts. "So, as you can

see on these pictures, we found this large mass in the large intestine."

"I remember you saying that! Mass! Blockage. Wow, it looks like it's blocking that whole tunnel almost."

"Yes, that 'tunnel' is your intestine, and this mass is almost completely obstructing it. That's what's been causing the pain, the odd stools, and recently the blood. I can't say this with 100% certainty, but I'm almost positive it's cancer. I wouldn't say that word if I wasn't sure. We've biopsied a piece and it's being tested and confirmed now, and we should have a result in a few days, but I would bet and plan on this being cancer."

Anna started crying. I said, "Cancer, huh? Well, that's okay, it's just another weird experience that will be a good story someday. Cancer's not so bad, it's not like it's... [struggling to think of the worst possible thing a doctor can tell you and coming up with] *CANCER*, or something." Anna cried harder. "I'll be fine, it'll be fine, this is all fine. That procedure was *bad*. This is fine, though, at least now we know." I remember really wanting to add: "and knowing is half the battle. GI JOE!" Anna didn't look like she would laugh at that right then, however.

This was January 19th, 2011, my friend Adrianna's 31st birthday and, oddly, 12 years to the day from my appendectomy. Adrianna is the main reason I graduated with a degree in biology. While we were taking every class together, she woke me up, dragged me to exams, and occasionally even forced me to study. We were roommates in the dorms. I lived with three women for a semester, four of us in one room, bunkbeds in a quad. I don't think any of our parents knew, but it was amazing, and not what you are picturing at all. Adrianna is like a sister to me, although everyone thought we were dating. She's barely 5 feet tall but always wore enormous platforms that we called "average height shoes", and was my fiercest defender since Sarah. We were the "punk rock biology kids" according to more than a couple professors – to be fair, we did both wear essentially the same clothes everyday (green army pants and black super holey/faded punk shirts) and had contests to see who could go longer without showering. Adrianna threw me a surprise 21st birthday party on the day of our organic chemistry final (which I failed in glorious fashion). Then, on her 31st birthday, I received a very different surprise and was diagnosed with colon cancer.

The next week was a blur of moments that don't feel like they really happened. My attitude towards the diagnosis was essentially pretending it wasn't happening and that it was going to be a minor inconvenience slowing me down for a few weeks, that's all. I chose not to tell a lot of people, only those who really needed to know. There was no calling old friends, healing old wounds, etc. I joked around about it a lot, making everyone very uncomfortable, then went about my life like it hadn't just completely changed forever – I went into work, I walked the dog, I made filming plans. I was having an issue with my agent at the time that was stressing me out as much as the diagnosis.

Telling my parents was terrible. My parents, Al and Maribeth Spain, are in my opinion the best parents in the world. I could not have had a better childhood, and that was in large part because of them. Mom told us that the most important thing in the world to her was being a mom – and she excelled at it. She not only allowed me to be the weirdo adventure-nature-kid, but encouraged it. She saw my passions and nurtured them, she helped me to not be afraid to be who I am, and to not let other people's hang-ups stop me from doing the things I love. Mom knows every kids' song, every kids' book, and every kids' activity ever created. She has one of each for every occasion and generally a recipe for a special meal to go along with them. She made three meals a day (plus snacks) for my entire childhood. Even when I was home on a break from college I could walk in the house at 2am and there would be a note on a plate of chicken parm saying, "Heat for 2 minutes and enjoy. I love you." And I never once, not for a second, doubted that love. I always knew that no matter what I did, how badly I messed up, she would always love and support me, which left me free to take a lot of chances and risks, and really to become who I am, knowing that love was always there.

Al has always led by example, showing me how to be a good person, rather than telling me. Almost every minute I spend with him is a lesson on it. Growing up, I observed the quiet humility with which he would enjoy a street musician, giving the person $5 we didn't have, but being so moved by the performance that he felt the guy deserved it for taking us out of ourselves for a few minutes while we watched and listened. He always put his family first – always. He never took advantage of anyone for any reason – if you saw a weakness in someone, you were to help them, not exploit it. Money isn't the most important thing in the world – compassion is. Al both hits all of the "dad" tropes and breaks them. First off, I call him Al, and always have. No one knows why. When I first started talking, everyone would refer to him as Pop or Poppy, and that's what Sarah calls him, but I would laugh and just call him Al. Everyone tried to get me to call him anything else but eventually gave up. All I would say in explanation was, "That's his name," and, because my mom is SUCH a mom, the logic never failed. Her name might be "Maribeth", but her real name is Mom. Even people who are not her kids call her Mom, and everyone calls Al, Al. It just works. So, yes, Al may have worn daisy dukes to cut the lawn, and he likes war documentaries, and always, always, *always*, to this day, will ask, "What route are you going to take?" when you tell him you're driving somewhere far away, but he also plays every instrument and was in a soul band when he was 16 (technically too young to be in most of the bars they performed in), makes his own golf clubs, guitars, and other instruments, and would sneak me in to punk clubs when I was in 7th grade. He has a gold tooth, and Sarah and I got him his first tattoo for his 50th birthday. It's "MSPN" in the ESPN logo, and he got it at Fun City Tattoo on St. Marks in the East Village the day I introduced him and Sarah to Anna. MSPN is "Maribeth, Sarah, Patrick, Nathan" – Nathan being my genius brother who is almost 13 years younger than me.

I could have phrased the cancer reveal a bit better in retrospect: "So, the good news is that we finally figured out why I've been getting all of those weird stomachaches and everything. The bad news is that I have cancer. Probably. The doctors think it's cancer, but I'll find out on Friday."

"So, it might not be cancer?" asked my crying mother, who lost her own mother and practically all her relatives to cancer.

"I guess it might not be, but it really probably is. We are moving forward assuming it's cancer." I stressed how the doctors thought this was going to be a straightforward laparoscopic surgery and easy recovery. They predicted I'd only be down for a couple of weeks post-surgery and then right back into the madness of my post-*Beast Hunter* season one life.

The formal diagnosis on the 21st was confirmation of what the doctors had assumed, and surgery was scheduled for the 31st. Instead of a sense of reality, the diagnosis brought more questions than answers, which would be a common theme for everything related to cancer from then on. It was cancer, and was at stage 2, or 3, or 4. I had to learn what the stages meant pretty quickly. It had probably metastasized at least a little, but they weren't completely sure. It probably didn't require chemo, but it might.

Despite having been around cancer my entire life – losing two grandparents to it and dozens of relatives and family friends – I realized right then that I didn't know too much about it. This epiphany came when I asked the doctor which was better – stage 2 or stage 4, then, after hearing their answer, I followed up with, "At least it's not stage 5." I had so much to learn. The main thing the doctors told me was: "Do not google any of this until we know more." It was great advice, and I was happy to follow it as this gave me a medically sanctioned way to further push this reality out of my mind.

On January 22 I was in NYC with Anna, Adrianna, and Adrianna's husband Jeremy (I had officiated their wedding a few months before in Bermuda) watching *American Idiot* on Broadway. Mike Dirnt happened to be in the crowd that night, and after the show he got up on stage and did a few Green Day songs with Billie Joe and some other cast members. It was an incredible weekend and just what I needed, but there was a cloud hanging over my head. I was trying to pretend like this wasn't weighing on me, but I was terrified. We got back to Boston and I spent the entire day on the 25th in a GI specialist's office learning about colon cancer and what my surgery would be like. I also had my first experience drinking barium and being injected with contrast dye before having a CT Scan – something I now look forward to as it always puts me to sleep and I have the rare chance to take an excused nap.

Anna and I took a sushi-making class on the 29th. Because I had spent the better part of the previous couple years working on *Beast Hunter*, I had booked a ton of stuff to make it up to Anna. Sushi making was on the 29th, a weekend trip to the White Mountains and a snowmobile lesson and tour was supposed to be February 5th, a snowboarding weekend was booked for the 12th, an 8 day trip to Italy, Greece, and Turkey was booked for February 15th-22nd (Anna's 30th birthday), a press tour that she was going to join me for was kicking off on the 25th, and a Nat Geo summit where I would be a featured speaker was on the 27th. The press tour would culminate with a premier of the series in DC at the Nat Geo headquarters on March 4th. Oh, we were also in the process of buying our first house, and were supposed to close on February 11th. It was going to be the best couple of months of our lives, capping what had already been the best year. Instead, I was sitting in a room where everything was a different shade of beige, in a hospital gown, learning what the stages of colon cancer were, and what treatment regimens were recommended for each.

My father came up to Boston and stayed with us so he could be there for the surgery on the 31st. I needed to do the same prep that you do for a colonoscopy on the 30th, so we planned a night in where I would be making frequent trips to the bathroom. My father rented the Helen Mirren/Bruce Willis movie *Red* because we all agreed we wouldn't mind missing parts of it and wouldn't really have to pay attention (probably the most honest assessment of why anyone would want to see that movie that it has received). Unfortunately, the movie had barely started when everything went to shit – or, to be more exact, did not go to shit. Because the tumor was almost entirely blocking my intestine, I wasn't able to complete the colon prep. I switched from the normal diarrhea to intense stomach pain to vomiting over the course of a couple of hours. I sweated through two outfits and defecated a ton of blood, but nothing else, before my father drove me to the hospital in the middle of the night. I couldn't sit in the car seat so I spent the 20 minute trip writhing on the floor of his backseat in agony while Anna rode shotgun. The hospital admitted me early, but the ER was not the same building as the surgery ward, so I was in an ambulance a few hours later headed down the road to the surgery hospital. I was on good drugs by that point, though.

The tumor had essentially closed off all points beneath it just as I'd taken medicine designed to make you evacuate everything from your system as quickly as possible, and all of that waste was hitting a brick wall. It would be like if every bathroom at the Boston Garden was down the same passageway, and they boarded up that hallway just as Mick announced, "Okay, we're going to play some of Keith's new stuff now."

I woke up – *after* the surgery this time – feeling great. A little groggy, a little sore, but cancer free for the first time in seven years! They had removed about six inches of my large intestine and 31 lymph nodes to look for spreading. Anna had organized some of our closest friends to come and visit me in the hospital, including Harry Marshall, the CEO of Icon Films. Harry brought me the only stylish silk scarf I have ever owned, a bunch of DVDs, including one of *Beast Hunter*, and a signed advance copy of Jeremy Wade's latest book, complete with a personalized, incredibly kind message from the man himself! I was feeling great and couldn't wait to get out of the hospital and back on track for the amazing things we had planned. We'd had to cancel the snowmobiling and snowboarding trips, and I was bummed that we'd lost the money on them. Despite what looks like a lavish lifestyle on paper, Anna and I were broke, and had been for years. She had a massive student-loan debt and I had spent six years bankrolling *Nature Calls*. *Beast Hunter* had paid better than I'd expected, but still only just about brought me up to zero in covering what I'd spent on *Nature Calls*. I'd been dodging calls from credit agencies the year before and had just raised my credit score enough to qualify for a high-interest loan for our first house. At least we'd still be able to go on the big 30th b-day trip I'd planned for Anna, and paid for with a non-refundable policy, and no insurance.

After that first surgery, I had a roommate, Kevin, during recovery. He was very nice – had a super kind partner and a daughter. He'd had an ostomy bag for the previous 10 years and had just had it removed and his intestines put back into his body. He was nervous, but excited. We talked about what his life had been like with the bag, how much he'd hated it at first but then come to appreciate what it was doing for him, and even love it – "The time I save wiping my ass every day! Man, that adds up!" He really cheered me up, and was the first of many survivors who let me know that life after this experience would be possible.

I was out of the hospital on February 4th, and by that evening I was bored and wanted to go out to eat. Anna convinced me it was a bad idea, and insisted she spend the next few days taking care of me. Al drove back to Wynantskill the next day, and I convinced Anna to go to work on the 6th and leave me in the apartment with our dog and cats. I said I felt fine and she should save her vacation days and join me on location for season 2 of *Beast Hunter*. She finally agreed and kissed me goodbye, leaving me as I made a stack of French toast that I planned on covering in butter and powdered sugar and eating by myself. I'd spent three years dieting for *Beast Hunter*, but I'd just beaten cancer and I was giving myself a cheat month. I shared the French toast with our pug, Sushi, and, feeling full and happy, decided to catch up on some e-mails.

I remember going from the kitchen to the guest bedroom where our computer setup was, getting up again to get some milk, getting halfway back to the kitchen, and collapsing in absolute agony. It was like someone had grabbed my testicles and squeezed them, then pulled them apart and away from my body. I fell to the ground and threw up from the pain, then thought, "Oh my God, I've fallen and I can't get up! Like those stupid commercials! I really have fallen, and I can't get up! This is so fucking dumb!" I started crying and laughing, and pulled myself to the bedroom where my phone was charging. Shaking, I called Anna, sobbing and apologizing. She asked if I needed to call 911 and then, suddenly, the pain was gone. GONE. As if it hadn't been there, like I'd imagined it. But nope, there was the milk and vomit, there was the drag-trail through the milk and vomit, and I was soaked through with sweat. What the actual fuck?

"Anna, I'm so sorry, I really feel better. I'm going to call the number the doctor gave me and try to... SHIT! MY BALLS!"

Anna, very confused, said: "Your balls? I thought you said you threw up and your stomach hurt."

"FUUUUUUUUUUUUUUUUUUUUUUUUUCK! MY BALLS! Ahhhhhhhhhhhgggg." I was laughing again.

"WHY ARE YOU LAUGHING?"

"OH MY GOD, I DON'T KNOW! WHAT IS HAPPENING? AHHHHHH MY BALLS! JESUUUUUUUSSSS! Please come home, please help me, I am so sorry, please help me, I am so sorry."

I was back to the floor, and by the time I'd gotten upright again, Anna was home (we worked at the same biotech company, and only lived about 15 minutes away). "I'm taking you to the ER," was all she said after determining I was conscious. By the time we'd gotten to the ER my testicles felt much better, but I did have a pretty terrible stomachache that seemed to be getting worse and worse. The doctors examined me and thought it was probably constipation. They gave me a bunch of laxatives and stool softeners and we waited while I was in agony. And then I shit my pants – the only time in my life that has ever happened. I was so angry. I was angry at myself, and the doctors, and everyone in the hospital. I was literally just standing there when I felt it happen. I looked at Anna and said, "Oh man, I think I just shit myself. Can you please leave?" I insisted on cleaning myself up, throwing my pants away, taking a shower at the hospital, and leaving after I pooped twice more, this time on the toilet.

I didn't talk on the way home. I wasn't embarrassed as much as just angry. I was not supposed to be 30 and shitting my pants in front of my girlfriend. How could she ever want to be with me after that? How could she look at me the same? This was not just stupid, it was unfair. This was supposed to be over. Cancer is like, so obnoxious and disruptive, you guys. Seriously though, I had no idea what was in store for me.

We got home, I apologized, and asked Anna to please go to work the next day. The only good thing about pooping in my pants was that I did feel better almost right away, and I got a free pair of scrubs. I wanted to sleep on the couch so that she could get some rest, I said – but really it was so that I could fume and get lost in my own anger and frustration, and not have to think about if she was looking at me with pity or thinking about me shitting my pants. Anna did not go to work the next day, but I just spent the day answering e-mails, planning the press tour, and doing over-the-phone interviews. We hadn't released any statement about cancer to the press, so pooping my pants didn't come up at all. My pain was pretty minimal, just the normal post-abdominal-surgery stuff. I wasn't going to do crunches for a while, but I was okay going up and down stairs, and could make my own food. By lunch we were joking about the pooping incident and I felt better all around. "I think you made the doctors nervous with all of that talk about your balls, and they gave you too much stool softener. If that's the worst thing that happens because you had cancer, then you're pretty lucky. Also, if that's the most embarrassing moment of your life, you're pretty lucky." Anna is very smart – did I mention that?

I slept in our bed that night and woke up feeling even better. I had a couple of articles to write and was looking forward to a late breakfast from this greasy-spoon diner in town that Anna and I loved. It was the only place we could afford when we first moved in together six years earlier, and we ate three meals a day there sometimes – which was hard, because they closed at 2pm. We had a low-key day at home. We played with Sushi, talked about the upcoming press tour, which stops Anna was going to join me on, when I'd be leaving my day job in biotech, and the new possibility of a trip to Australia before the series started airing there in May. It was an incredible and healing day – one I'd really needed.

The next, the 8th, was not a good day – in fact, it was possibly the worst day of my life up to that point. One of the most amazing things about cancer is, you get diagnosed, and you feel like that's the worst day of your life, but it isn't. That target keeps getting lower and lower and lower. On the 8th, I once again convinced Anna to go back to work. She was working

2nd shift so we had a nice morning together before she left, and then I was once again in agony, feeling as if my testicles were being ripped from my body. I called her, and she called our downstairs neighbors who were in their 80s and couldn't drive at night. Anna once again raced home and brought me to the ER in what was starting to feel like an all-too-familiar routine. This time, the pain did not let up, and I was shaking and sweating at the ER. After being admitted I somehow convinced Anna to go home. As dumb as it sounds, I think I was worried about pooping my pants again and didn't want her there if it happened. I told her this was likely going to be a long week and asked her to please leave me and get some sleep. I told her I loved her and that there was nothing she could do there, just sleep, and I'd call her if anything changed. The doctors did a CAT scan which revealed nothing. It was blurry because I couldn't stop shaking, but didn't raise any red flags. They gave me a bunch of meds, including lorazepam, and left me in one of those ER "rooms" that is really just a bed with four curtains in a hallway. They thought it was probably gas pains.

Another patient in that hallway was a young woman from the Caribbean, her husband, and her mother. As I lay there, feeling sorry for myself, I couldn't help but overhear their conversation. A very kind doctor was explaining to the woman that her child had succumbed to SIDS and there was nothing they could do. She was wailing, "My baby! My baby! Bring back my baby!"

"I'm so sorry, ma'am. There's nothing we could do. He was already dead when you arrived here. There are no words I can say right now to make this better other than you did everything you could. Take as much time as you need. We'll bring your baby back to you now." And the whole family was just in hysterics, talking about what a beautiful baby he was and how special and how could this happen? Why this baby? How could the doctors not do anything? And I was lying there feeling like a piece of shit. I felt like a piece of shit for overhearing this, for being in the same place as they were. I felt like a piece of shit for thinking anything I was going through mattered compared to what they were going through. I felt like a piece of shit for how angry and frustrated I'd been the other day in the hospital, and how frustrated I was even an hour ago when the doctors couldn't figure out what was happening with me, and for anything self-centered I'd ever done in my life. For every first-world problem I'd ever complained about. I mostly felt like a piece of shit for just being there, in pain, knowing that my physical pain couldn't touch the pain they felt, and that all three of them would have gladly swapped places with me. I lay there and cried, listening to this young family cradle, cry, and coo over their dead child, for three hours. And I felt like a piece of shit because it was the worst thing I had ever experienced and I wasn't even the one experiencing it.

The next day I didn't feel much better, but the doctors said they had no reason to keep me and would have to discharge me. I was so emotionally numb that I didn't even try to fight it. I did mention that my stomach was still aching and my testicles felt like they were being kicked into my stomach, but agreed that sure, that could be gas pain, what the fuck did I know? I took the meds and prescriptions they gave me, called Anna, and went home. I didn't tell Anna about the previous night. (In fact, the first time she heard about it was when she read an early draft of this chapter.) I just told her I was exhausted, it had been a terrible night, and I wanted to sleep while she filled the prescriptions. My condition was going downhill fast, and when she got back from filling the prescription I was lying in a pool of sweat on our bed unable to talk because the pain was so intense. Anna called the doctor and explained what was happening, and they explained that it was a normal reaction to post-abdominal surgery. Another hour went by and Anna noticed that my stomach seemed to be swelling and I wasn't really able to focus or have a coherent conversation. She called the doctor again and they were concerned, but felt that it didn't warrant another trip – the third in just a few days – and said maybe I had a mild infection, and that one of my prescriptions should take care of it. When I started vomiting green stuff and my stomach swelled so much it looked like I was pregnant, Anna wasn't taking "no" for an answer and drove me to the ER.

Chapter 4

"Do Not, and Do Not Let Anyone Else, Insert Anything into Your Stoma"

I don't remember the ride to the hospital at all. The next thing I remember after vomiting what looked like pea soup and tasted like battery acid all over the bathroom in our apartment is vomiting what looked like pea soup and tasted like battery acid all over someone who was trying to shove an intubation tube down my throat at the hospital. My vomiting and apologizing surprised them as much as it surprised me, as did my questions of, "Where am I? What is happening?" They tried intubating me again, with the same results. "Why do I look pregnant? Oh God, it hurts. It hurts so bad. Someone please kill me. Please kill me. Please make this stop. Anna, I'm so sorry, I love you. Please make this stop." Then I was out – out-out, in a medically induced coma for four days.

I'm told my parents came out and raged at the doctors and entire medical team. They cried with Anna and Adrianna. They stayed at our apartment and took shifts at the hospital. They watched bad movies and ate pizza and Panera. They yelled at the doctors some more, and cried some more. Anna fielded calls from concerned friends and loved ones. She deflected those who wanted to visit (aside from Adrianna), and kept our friends at Icon and biotech up to date with what was happening. She took personal unpaid leave from work and kept our animals alive. She dropped Sushi off at our friend Brian's house after he volunteered to watch him for as long as we needed. She kept our lives together, while I was sort of dead.

After four days, the hospital staff woke me up. My only memory of that time is the color purple – not the book or movie, the actual color purple. I remember everything being purple, which wasn't so bad. Nothing hurt, nothing bothered me, I didn't know anything other than the color purple, which felt peaceful and good. It's one of my favorite colors. When I opened my eyes, purple morphed into hospital beige and the pain immediately flooded into reality, and my first words were not, "I love you, Anna, Mom and Al, thank you," or, "I'm sorry to put everyone through this." They were, "Hello, oh no, oh God. Fuck. This really hurts." I started crying, "Please make this stop. Please put me back to sleep. Please put me under. Please, this really hurts. Oh God, what is this thing in my side? Oh no, shit, please make this stop. Put me under. Why did you wake me up?" Everything hurt. Everything.

It turned out that the pain in my balls was an unexpected result of my intestines flipping. The best the doctors could guess is that it was intense abdominal pain that I couldn't associate with anything other than getting kicked in the balls, so, for some reason that's how it felt to me. It also could have been some weird crossed nerves. They don't know for sure but said these kind of injuries resulted in absolutely horrific intense pain that anyone experiencing it seemed to express in different ways.

And now, a short anatomy lesson – your intestines move, a lot. As they move your food down through them, they wiggle and shake and bounce and jostle against other squishy organs in there. Occasionally they get a little too jumpy and flip or twist, which for most people means they have to lie down for a while in incredible pain while their intestines right themselves. If they don't right themselves, a blockage forms at the twist-point and the person needs some medical intervention to untwist them and let everything flow again. If you are lucky enough to have this happen in the right place shortly after a surgery to remove a portion of your intestines, like me, then the weak point rips open after twisting and all of the literal shit in your intestines spills out into your body cavity – just floating around in there poisoning you from the inside. I had gone septic. I had to be cut open from my sternum to my penis and have surgeons essentially give my insides a shower. My organs had to be exposed to air and flushed with saline, then, when I was clean on the inside, I was left open for four days because the swelling was so severe that they couldn't sew me back up. Also, that "filling my body cavity with literal shit" was so traumatic that I needed a few additional things put in before closing me up.

I had to have two drain tubes put in my sides – a big one, which was about as big around as my pinkie finger, and a little one, that was about the size of the tubing from a fish-tank air rock. Drain tubes are exactly what they sound like – rubber tubes inserted into actual holes in my sides with stitches placed around and crisscrossing over them to keep them from moving too much or accidentally pulling out or poking in further than they needed to be. A constant stream of pinkish-grey, thick, and foul-smelling liquid dripped from these tubes into collecting bags. This was bacteria draining out of my body as my immune system forced it away from vital organs. The tubes hurt as bad as you'd imagine two things sticking deep into your abdominal tissue would. The stitches pulled and kept tearing and bleeding or oozing every time I breathed or moved, and even the slightest shift in my weight caused stabbing pains at the insertion sites. I developed bedsores from staying in one position so long because I was so afraid of disturbing the tubes if I even moved an inch to adjust my weight. The little one was taken out after a few days, but the big one was in for over a week.

I also had to have non-dissolvable stitches for a number of the surgical wounds because my immune system was so off that it could have either dissolved the stitches too quickly or sent me into shock because they would be one thing too many for it to deal with. These still bother me to this day. I had feeding and breathing tubes, the latter of which came out almost at once after I woke up, and I remember watching it and being surprised by how long it was. The former needed to stay in for a couple weeks. I lost 35 pounds in the hospital and looked a little like Christian Bale in *The Machinist* by the end of it. Saving the best for last – I had an ileostomy. Essentially, they split my large intestine and pulled it out of a hole in my stomach about an inch away from where my belly button used to be (which was cut through for the "open him up and clean him out" portion of the show). The intestines that were poking out looked disturbingly like a red sea squirt.

I knew, intellectually, that the angry red sea squirt sticking out of my stomach was also saving my life, but I hated it. I hated it so much. I didn't want to look at it, I didn't want to acknowledge that it was there, I didn't want to learn about it. I noticed it almost immediately after waking up, and the only thing I could think to say was, "Oh no, no-no-no, that's not supposed to be there. The doctors told me I didn't need one of those. Why is that there?" I hate thinking about it too much even now.

When I first woke up, after begging to be put back to sleep, the doctors were visibly excited that I was coherent, which should have been my first clue that things had gone really poorly after the *Exorcist*-style pea-soup vomit. They started explaining things to me and it was a crazy amount of information to receive all at once. They told me I'd been out for four days, which seemed impossible to me. Four days? I lost four days? How could I be this tired if I'd been asleep for four days? How could I feel this terrible and be in this much pain? They told me I'd had a major operation and my scars would more significant than from my first surgery. Then they told me I had a Patient Controlled Analgesia (PCA) pump, which meant I could give myself a shot of morphine when I needed it by clicking the button they put in my hand. Then I sort of stopped listening because I heard "morphine" and immediately started clicking like it was the TV remote of someone whose mom had just walked in the room while they were watching porn. The doctor said, "It records every click, but there is a minimum amount of time that must pass before it actually administers a dose." I was clicking away, still barely listening. Then they asked me to not pull at the tubes I was pulling at – oxygen and feeding – and explained the drain tubes, which I had absolutely no desire to pull at as even the slightest movement brought sharp stabbing pains. They hurt when I talked. They hurt when I breathed. Within five minutes of being awake, the doctors had put on gloves and repositioned the big tube, removing and adding more stitches around a gaping hole in the side of my stomach. After that minor surgery, I was at least able to think and focus. I was still clicking away at the PCA though, telling myself that some of the clicks must be giving me morphine.

They then moved on to the bag. "Pat, I know you weren't expecting this, but let me explain…" They went on to tell me how much trauma I'd experienced, and how there was no way my intestines were up to the job right now. "We don't believe it will be permanent – we could reverse it in a few months, or a year, or a couple of years depending on how things progress. We'll go over care and maintenance tomorrow, once you've had a rest." My mind went back to Kevin, my roommate from right after the first surgery – 10 years of having this thing in his stomach. I couldn't imagine ever appreciating it. I hated it so much. It represented not being who I'd been – not having the freedom I had taken for granted. How could I travel with this? How could I stay in pygmy villages with this? How could I be shirtless on camera? How could I ever be spontaneous about anything again when I needed to always have these supplies, and clean conditions, and how could I have sex or experience any form of intimacy? How could I possibly expect Anna to be able to look past this and actually feel some sense of desire for me when there is actual shit coming out of my stomach at random times. What if it leaked? How could I do *anything* with this? Oh God, I needed more morphine. I didn't want to think,

I didn't want to be there. I knew it wasn't the worst thing in the world – I had overheard the worst thing in the world a few days before, and still felt sick even being upset about anything other than that. But this was the worst thing in *my* world.

There is a line from the song *People II 2: Still Peoplin'* by the band AJJ, which is about depression and the terrible things you experience or witness in life, which brings me back to that moment:

You don't have it any better.
You don't have it any worse.
You're an irreplaceable human soul with your own understanding of what it means to suffer
And that's a huge bummer.

Credit: *People II 2: Still Peoplin'* reproduced by permission of AJJ and Terrorbird Publishing, LLC

That seems to sum it up. I was suffering in a way unique to my situation, which was making it almost impossible to move on from that suffering.

I asked the doctors why they couldn't have kept me in a coma until there was no need for the bag. Anna started crying. It was a new low for me, and a moment of selfishness that hurts to admit now. But I hated everything right then. From the ostomy bag, they went on to the catheter in my penis. They told me they were going to take it out, and that if I didn't pee on my own in a couple hours they'd have to put it back in. Spoiler alert – that catheter came out and went in five or six more times over the next week. I went from a comfortable place of "I can't remember ever having something stuck into my penis" to "Oh, this again" very quickly. Any time the catheter was out, I had a weirdly phallic-looking bottle that I was supposed to lay on the bed and pee into. It almost invariably necessitated my asking for help from a nurse and/or spilling pee all over the place, usually at

2am. You stop thinking about it at some point. There was one night I was so frustrated with the entire process and in so much pain from moving around while positioning the bottle, and I really didn't want to have the fucking catheter put back in, that I just sat in a puddle of urine for a few hours before I gathered the strength, mental and physical, to tell a nurse.

They then went over a ton of logistical information I mostly didn't hear, although I nodded and stared, and asked me if I wanted to sign a power of attorney and assign a medical proxy – I did both with Anna. I tried to make a joke that this was even better than a marriage license, but it didn't translate from my now gloriously morphine-flooded brain. After about an hour had passed, the doctors checked my PCA log and said, "Well, you've administered four doses of morphine in the last hour and have clicked the PCA... 752 times. I think we will up your dose if that's o–"

"YES," was my response, not letting them finish, and then, thankfully, I was given a large dose and fell asleep.

I woke up, and it was all real. All of this shit had actually happened. I had an ostomy bag, bandages covering my entire stomach, tubes up my nose, in my sides, in my penis, my arms, my hands, tape everywhere, and I couldn't move without horrible pain. Oh, there's a button in my hand (click-click-click-click)... hmmm, that's a little bit better. Anna and my parents were there, and told me the doctors and a social worker wanted to talk to me about the ostomy. Excellent, my favorite subject. I told them I didn't want to talk about it. Everyone got really quiet and said that I needed to.

The team of doctors came in and handed me a pamphlet about the bag that I immediately handed to Anna, and told them I didn't want to read it. I think I said, "Everything is blurry and I can't read it," which wasn't true, I just really didn't want to.

Then they told me, "The pamphlet will go over everything..." at which point my attention drifted and I nodded, not really listening, and took the pamphlet back from Anna so I could realistically pretend to be paying attention. I opened it and the first thing I read was, "So do not, and do not let anyone, insert your/their penis, fingers, or anything else into your stoma."

What the actual fuck? "Do people try to have sex with other people's stomas?" I asked, cutting off the doctor as they were probably explaining something important.

"Ummmm... is that a concern of yours?"

"I mean, that's literally the first thing this pamphlet says. Who would see this and think, 'Yeah, that sounds good'."

"Pat, you have to understand – most people who have these are in a desperate situation."

I tried to put the thoughts of someone having sex with someone else's stoma out of my head, but it was not easy. I was just staring at this pulsating, jerky sea creature jutting out of my previously smooth side, occasionally spewing brownish-green fluid into a clear bag, and I couldn't stop thinking about the fact that some people wanted to have sex with this thing, and I would probably never have sex again because I would never stop thinking about it being there, filling a bag that was bees-waxed to my stomach with my shit.

I paid enough attention to get a basic understanding of how to change, clean, and maintain it. I tried to pretend it was an academic study, and tried to think about how truly remarkable it was and scientifically fascinating, but I failed. I hated it. I hated that Anna had to be there to learn how to take care of it also. I promised her that I would NEVER ask her to change the bag, clean it, or look at it. She told me to shut up, and I broke that promise pretty quickly in any case. I couldn't do anything on my own.

My parents told me that I had a roommate for the first few days I was out of the coma. I have absolutely no recollection of him at all. They tell me he was really nice, around my age, with incredibly kind and loving parents, and terminal cancer. Al said that it was hard for them to think about, but it was nice to talk to him and his parents. In those first few days, these parents, whose son was going to die from cancer in the very near future, seemed more positive and had a better outlook than my parents or Anna, and none of them knew what to make of that. I have not been able to bring myself to ask any more about him, or why he stopped being my roommate after a few days. We all have our own understanding of what it means to suffer.

Chapter 5

"Your Butthole Doesn't Remember How to Close"

The next four to five weeks were a blur of misery and insanity. I was in and out of a morphine-induced haze. Day and night had no meaning other than how many back-to-back episodes of *Pawn Stars* and *Storage Wars* I could watch. I couldn't eat or drink anything for the first three weeks, and all I wanted was a glass of water. Anna and my parents were amazing, and there every day. Adrianna came to visit a lot and a few other friends came a couple of times, but I was terrible company. If I was coherent enough to actually have a conversation, I was too in my own head to really have that conversation. Most of the time, I was just clicking the button on the PAC and escaping into morphine.

Each day consisted of regular temperature and glucose checks, having my fingers pricked every four hours, having my bedsores treated by a nurse rolling me on my side while another changed bandages as I tried not to scream from the pain of moving, dealing with my ostomy – or, more honestly, not dealing with it and asking the amazing nursing staff to change the bag when it needed it, and having someone ask me every four hours for my name and birthday, how I felt and how much pain I was in on a scale of 1 to 10. There were funny moments as well. Anna has a video of me sitting in bed with my eyes closed "fishing". I'm casting a line, reeling it in slowly, casting again and smiling. You can hear my father say in the background, "At least he looks happy," and I do. I look terrifyingly skinny – but happy. I'm normally around 175-185 pounds – I was down to 130. I hadn't weighed 130 pounds since 5th grade.

I was given the final "stage" rating of my cancer one day, and – surprise – it wasn't good news. Three of the 31 lymph nodes they removed showed signs that the cancer had metastasized. That, along with the fact that the tumor had actually penetrated the wall of my intestine, meant a diagnosis of stage 3 – which meant I had chemo to look forward to, and, statistically speaking, a 50% chance of surviving the next five years. The doctors assured me that those statistics were skewed and made the outlook seem worse than it probably was. Most people with stage 3 colon cancer are elderly and in poor health in other ways. There are no stats for otherwise healthy 30-year-olds with it, but they assured me the outlook was probably much better. They "fully expected" me to be alive in five years. That did not make me feel great – even having a conversation about being alive in five years was surreal – much less the reality that, according to math, I only had a 50% chance at it.

I woke up in a panic in the middle of one night because suddenly I wasn't in the hospital but an Italian specialty store, and there were dried meats and cheeses hanging from the ceiling all around my bed. I could see it so clearly. I pushed the panic button and a nurse came running in. I immediately blurted out, "Why is there so much ham in here?" in a terrified voice. The nurse wasn't sure what was happening, and I repeated, "So. Much. Ham. Look around." As I looked around I started seeing the hospital room as it really was, alongside aspects of the Italian store too. A random shelf with anise cookies and Jordan almonds, a cooler with sausages and meatballs, an IV machine with a bunch of bags, and a shelf of medical supplies. I was very confused and dizzy. To their credit, the nurse just reassured me that I was safe, and this was normal, and I should try to rest. They said they'd call Anna and tell her my concerns about the ham, and what had happened with the room changing to a store and back again. They kept a completely straight face, and did call Anna, who was there 30 minutes later even though it was 2 or 3am.

One day we bought a house. Have I mentioned that I'm

55

stubborn? I refused to let this experience stand in the way of progress and, after spending a year looking at what felt like hundreds of homes, we finally found one we really liked and could afford, in a location we were excited about. I was not going to let cancer or ruptured intestines stand in the way of that. I had signed power of attorney over to Anna a few days before this in the presence of a lawyer and a cowboy. (The cowboy probably wasn't there, but he seemed very real, and was excited about the house.) Anna had to wake me up a few times to sign. The doctors in the room just nodded and said, after getting to know me a bit, they felt like this was the right move. And it absolutely was. By the end of the day, we had officially set a closing date for the house – I just needed to be much more coherent in about nine weeks. Anna never mentioned the very real possibility that I wouldn't be there in five years, but I mentioned it – along with the statement: "Thanks to my insurance policy, I'm worth way more dead than alive, so you'll be all set with the house if I don't make it." I honestly thought that might make her feel better about this life-changing purchase. It did not.

My niece was born on February 12th, and my mom missed the birth because she was in the hospital with me. A few days later, Al and Anna convinced her to go to New Jersey and be with her daughter and new grandchild, and they would stay with me. And they did – they stayed through the hallucinations, rages, sullen silences, and endless explanations about how *Pawn Stars* and *Storage Wars* were maybe the best shows ever made.

There was one night in there when I really gave up. I was absolutely convinced that I would never be normal again – at least, as normal as a guy who willingly seeks out venomous animals can be considered. It was a terrible night. I was fighting off some secondary infection and having a reaction to one of the pain meds and surgical tape. My entire body was itchy, even my face, and it was so frustrating because it hurt so much to move. It was around midnight and suddenly I had to poop. I had a bag on my stomach that was supposed to be taking care of that – how could I have to poop if my intestines were split and pulled out of my stomach? Fun fact about ostomies – the bit between your stoma and rectum doesn't really know it's not on duty anymore, and it's still absorbing some stuff, processing it, and producing "feces", which would really just be a ball of dead bacteria. So, the doctors excitedly told me that this meant my organs were trying to work and that was a good thing. Oh yay. I could barely contain my excitement.

In order to pass this ball of dead bacteria, I had to get out of bed for the first time. My muscles had atrophied, my bedsores were oozing and bleeding, there were wires and tubes going everywhere, and I had spent the past couple weeks doing everything in my power to not move at all, and suddenly it was imperative that I get to a bathroom. Anna and the night nurse spent a very awkward 15 minutes getting me to a toilet. I was bleeding, crying, stumbling – but I was not going to poop in the bed, as the nurse first suggested, even making a little nest of towels for me. I was NOT going to do that. So, there I sat on the toilet, swaying, for 45 minutes while the last bit of my intestines did what it could to remove the last vestige of any pride along with those bacterial cells.

After shaking, sweating, yelling in pain, and being forced to give a blow-by-blow account of what was happening through the door because I wouldn't let Anna or the nurse into the room, I finally passed a small, black/green, terrible smelling rock-hard stone the size of a large grape. I was so relieved that I started laugh-crying. Then it was time to wipe, and wipe, and wipe, and wipe and flush, and wipe more. Twenty minutes later, Anna tentatively asked if everything was okay.

"Fine, just fine – I'll be out in a minute I think." Twenty minutes later, nearly 2am, the roll of toilet paper was gone and I was no closer to having cleaned up, I finally had to speak up.

I explained the situation to the nurse, who went and got a

doctor, who then explained through the door, loudly, "Your, um, your butthole, doesn't remember how to close. The best you can do is use a warm wet towel to clean a little more, then just sit on towels for the next few days and we'll see if it remembers what it needs to do." Jesus Christ, where is rock bottom in this situation? Because I kept thinking I'd hit it, and then there was more.

That night, clicking away at the PCA, lying on towels because my butthole couldn't close, with a stoma filling an ostomy bag on the other side, drain tubes in both of my sides, and wires and IVs coming from all parts of my arms and hands, my lips cracked and bleeding from dehydration, my fingers bruised and scabbed from constant glucose testing, watching my 15th episode of *Pawn Stars* – I thought: "This is it. This is my life, if I even survive. This is it, and what is this? Why do I even want this? There is a good chance I'm going to die from either the cancer coming back or these infections, and if by some chance I don't die, this is what I have now. I'm a burden to everyone I love, I'm terrible to be around, I'm in constant pain, and perpetually in impossibly embarrassing and dehumanizing situations." I saw absolutely no light at the end of any tunnel and collapsed into a morphine sleep, not really thinking or caring about waking up again.

A couple of nights later, Anna expressed concerns to the doctors regarding my dependence on morphine. She asked me first, and I said, "But I need it, I can't imagine being alive without morphine. It is quite literally the only way that I can make it through a day." After talking to my doctors and telling them what she was seeing, they agreed that it was time to ease me off it. The next day was hell as I went through full-on withdrawal. I sweated through two mattresses, screaming in agony and frustration, the drain tube bleeding because I was writhing around in pain, and Anna was there, apologizing and second guessing herself. She shouldn't have – she'd been right,

I was fully addicted and needed to stop before I could even look at recovering.

I know what I was going through, but I can't imagine what she felt. She was feeling guilt, and sympathy, and anger, and frustration, and more guilt – so much guilt. She knew this was the right call, but seeing the effect was pushing her to the breaking point. She'd been with me through all of this – all of it. More so than anyone else, she knew the full ramifications and how far I'd truly fallen. I still can't believe she stuck with me. When I hear stories of a partner who left their significant other during some phase of their treatment for a debilitating disease, I think that person is often judged way too harshly. People say, "Can you believe they would do that? Well, that's really showing your true colors." Yes, I can believe it. And no, no it isn't "showing your true colors." It's showing that you are a human who can't stand seeing a person you love become something so different from that. I say it and I mean it in every sense of the word – I am in awe that Anna stayed. I would feel no ill will if she hadn't. I would understand. No one knows if they can be as strong as she was in that situation. It's unfathomable if you aren't in it. She stayed, and, writing this 10+ years later, I'm still grateful and amazed.

I've described my withdrawal as, "*Trainspotting* without the baby crawling on the ceiling," and that feels pretty right. Opioid addiction is no joke, and I only had a taste of it. In a few weeks, I was mentally and physically addicted and needed a lot of support to break it. I had an amazing support system in all aspects of my life, and it was still hell. I have the utmost respect for anyone dealing with addiction in any form who is able to live another day without satisfying that urge. Again, we as a society judge addicts far too harshly. This was not something I could recognize or break free of on my own, and again, I have the best possible scenario for a support system and life outside of this situation.

The day after was a little easier, and the day after that a little better. Three days after morphine and I was feeling more like myself. About a week later, I had pooped again and my butthole remembered how to do its job. I was also able to drink water and eat clear liquids! You have never in your life tasted anything as good as that first sip of water after having nothing to drink for weeks. The next day, Anna, who continually surprised me with how awesome she was in every possible way in every situation, surprised me with some Italian ice from a local ice cream place we loved. Blue vanilla and bubblegum. My thinking in regards to Italian ice is that, if you are going to eat something artificial, it should be the most outrageously artificial version of that thing possible – hence the flavor choices. Screw water – THIS was the best thing I had ever tasted. From that day on, every day, Anna would wait outside the doors until the place opened to get me a different Italian ice flavor.

Now I was feeling a bit more human, the doctors and nursing staff were starting to get to know me – the actual me, not the me of the last month. They would tell me when they'd seen ads for *Beast Hunter* on TV, or bring me magazines with interviews I'd given months before finally being published. They also joked with me and told me some of the crazy things I'd done on morphine (like the ham story). They were amazed because, apparently, I was the only patient they'd ever had in the ICU who never rated their pain at a "10". They said, "Even the absolute worst pain, when we could see you were in agony, you could barely speak and all you could say were one word answers – usually 'morphine' or 'fuck' – you would only give yourself an 8 or 9 through clenched teeth. Everyone gives us one 10, at least."

I replied, "Yeah, let me tell you about bullet ants." The Amazonian bullet ant ceremony is a 10, and the only 10 I hope to ever experience. (For reference, the bullet ant ceremony is a 10, having your intestines rupture and go septic is a 9, kidney stones are a hard 8, and although I am physiologically unable to give birth I hear that is up there. In my experience, nothing else even comes close.)

Anna's 30th birthday was February 22 and we were supposed to be in Turkey. Instead, we were in a hospital room. That morning, the nurses had helped procure some art supplies for me from the pediatric cancer ward (one of the worst word combinations in the English language) so that, like a six-year-old on Mother's Day, I could make her a card. I chose a purple marker and drew her a picture of a cat licking its butt – which was not only an inside joke, but felt very appropriate based on what we'd been going through – and wrote her a completely insufficient note about how amazing she was, how much I loved her, and how I would do everything in my power to make sure every birthday she had from then on was incredible.

For my 30th the previous May, Anna planned a huge amazing party at an Italian restaurant in our town with all of our friends and family. It was a wonderful day, and one we still talk about often. We don't talk about Anna's 30th very much. It was a hard day. Making the card had taken up a lot of my energy, and I'd hoped to demonstrate my new ability of walking nearly all the way down the hallway that I'd been practicing, but when Anna was there I could only make it to the nurse's station, which frustrated me. She told me it was fine, and that she loved the card. But it was not fine – I was a 30-year-old who was trying to impress his girlfriend and show her how hard I'd been working with a construction paper and marker card, and mastering the skill of "walking down a hallway". It was absolutely not fine. A couple of weeks after that, however, I left the hospital.

"Embarrassing and dehumanizing" is how I describe my hospital stay in my various talks – three words that simultaneously do a great job summing it up and failing to fully convey what it was like. Nor can the hundreds of words I've written that you've just read. I am not easily embarrassed, but this was humiliating. I was regularly sitting in bed, naked, and nurses would come in unannounced and just move my penis to the side in order to check on various tubes, drains, etc. I was urinating in a container in bed – which often required help, getting sponge baths, suppositories, discussing poop, pee, and gas with strangers. I had a room of strangers applaud when I passed gas during a conversation, and in the moment I was happy about it too – ecstatic in fact. Ten seconds later I wanted to cry because I was being treated, and felt like, a toddler. The worst part was having all of this happen in front of Anna, and her necessarily being involved in some of it.

Dehumanizing is the word for it – becoming "less than human". When I think about what defines a human, what our society has agreed upon to call ourselves "human" – this experience took that away from me. I felt less than, and it was terrible. Bodily functions and the functions of life are a very small, but essential, part of who we are, but during those weeks, that was all I was. I was not a person with a personality, emotions, loves, passions, interests, and goals, I was a collection of biological functions that could be charted, checked, and compared to a control. I was not a person, I was an organism. Leaving the hospital, I started to become a person again.

I was in and out of the hospital a few more times over the next two months. Dozens of surgeries had happened and would continue to happen during that time – picc lines, drain tubes went in and out and in and out, stitches in and out, a port put in for chemo, IVs, catheters, suppositories, feeding tubes, etc. From the time I went into the hospital for the first time on January 30th, it was about eight weeks of some of the lowest lows I've ever felt in my life, but, once I was home, I started feeling human again. Sushi came back to live with us and cheered me up, as did visits from friends and family. I regained the ability to walk by having Anna drive us to a 24-hour grocery store late at night and using a shopping cart to prop myself up as I walked the aisles.

I ate anything I wanted – which sometimes meant two pound bags of M&Ms, or an entire batch of cookies – to regain weight. (Which I eventually did – and then some. By the end of the year I was up over 185 pounds, which meant it was probably time to slow down on the M&Ms.) By the end of March, I was looking at surgery to finally reverse the ostomy and put my intestines back on the inside where they belonged.

Chapter 6

"You Missed Season 2"

Beast Hunter premiered a couple of days after I was discharged from hospital. It premiered without my having done any in-person promotions – I did not go on *The Tonight Show* like I was supposed to, or *Ellen*, or travel to major cities to appear on news programs. I was not interviewed on *Today*, nor able to make in-person appearances at the Nat Geo world conferences and give a talk. Nor did I attend either premier party in England or Washington DC. *Beast Hunter* premiered with me on my couch, with Anna, Adrianna, Adrianna's father, and Anna's cousins in attendance. I was supposed to "live chat" with fans during the show, so I didn't really even watch it. Harry and Laura had bought me a new MacBook Pro as a thank you and get-well gift – and an amazing gift it was! I started writing these books on that laptop. But it was newly arrived that morning, and I was still getting used to it.

In addition to the MacBook, I had sunglasses and shoes from Timberland that I still wear, ten+ years later, wine, snacks, and keepsakes from the series from Icon, and an amazing array of Nat Geo merch, DVDs, and gourmet foods from the network. Everyone was so good to me, and I will never forget their kindness and the way it made me feel they were still thinking of me, after I had written myself off.

I didn't feel the way I expected to feel seeing my first TV series' premier. It was exciting, but it also reminded me of all of the things I had missed and couldn't do in the short term, and might never be able to do again, assuming I was alive in the long term. I was and remain incredibly proud of the series, and loved seeing it on TV – but it was with mixed emotions that I watched those first two episodes and responded to people I'd never met on Twitter talking about something that had taken up nearly three years of my life.

The show was well received and rated pretty well. I was recognized a couple of times on my nightly grocery-store walks, and people told me they really liked the show and hoped I was feeling better. I'm not 100% sure when, but at some point in the hospital Anna and I had let Nat Geo and everyone involved in the show know about my diagnosis. Everyone was incredibly supportive and told me we could go public with it or not – it was 100% my decision. I thought that if the knowledge of what I was going through helped anyone with what they were going through, then it was worth any discomfort I felt talking about it, so I did an interview with the *Boston Globe* that focused on my cancer story up to that point. It was picked up pretty widely and I received a number of calls from different cancer-survivor organizations to ask if I'd speak to other people, especially young adults, who were going through the same thing as me. I wholeheartedly agreed.

My friend Barny, the series producer for *Beast Hunter*, recommended that I reach out to the American Cancer Society and offer my skills and platform – he thought my talking about it publicly would make me feel better, and he was absolutely right. I started speaking at ACS Relay for Life events, then some of their national events, and then their political-action committee ACS CAN and a young-adult focused survivor-support group, Stupid Cancer. I really threw myself into it and got more out of each talk than I probably gave to the crowd. I spoke a couple of times on my way to chemo, and a couple of others just a day or two after when I felt like absolute garbage, but the act of speaking gave me so much strength and hope. Meeting with survivors at these talks helped me feel normal as well, and helped me start to hope that I actually could get past this. Their stories showed me I wasn't alone, and that other people before me had beaten this disease.

I made some great friends in ACS and really found my people in Stupid Cancer. It was amazing to be around people who truly "got it", who would laugh at the horrifically dark jokes I would make and talk openly about the crazy shit running through my head 24/7. It made me feel less crazy, and let me know I was far from alone in my experiences. I loved wearing my "Stupid Cancer" T-shirt and bracelets, and having them spark a random conversation with a stranger – a person who was going through it themselves, or had a family member who was. Letting them know they were not alone helped me as much as it helped them, I think.

I was getting stronger physically and mentally as the weeks went by and the commercials and series kept airing and gaining new fans. I received encouraging e-mails and social-media messages from fans and cancer survivors, and folks who had lost people to cancer. I really felt I was connecting with this community and *Beast Hunter* was giving me a platform to reach a lot of people with my story.

A couple of weeks after the 5th and final episode of the series aired, I received a message on my answering machine from one of the heads of Nat Geo telling me he was so excited that they'd just renewed for season 2, and as soon as I was strong enough he'd love to see me at their headquarters in DC to celebrate. I was elated. I called my family and friends, Anna and I celebrated by splurging on takeout, and I started allowing myself to think about and look forward to the future.

That was a Friday morning. On Monday, I found out Nat Geo had gone through some major organization changes Friday afternoon, and the person who had called me no longer worked there. It was a few weeks of chaotic back-and-forths before we received the final answer that, in fact, *Beast Hunter* was not being renewed. It was a setback, and I was sad, but I had accomplished my dream of making a series for Nat Geo, and I was still beaming from that. Also, as an organization, they had been so incredibly amazing that there was absolutely nothing but positive feelings from me towards them. I love Nat Geo – always have and always will. This was not a personal decision. Everyone involved in *Beast Hunter* was incredible, and many are still friends to this day.

So, I wasn't doing series 2, but I was doing chemo, which was much more my focus than anything TV related. It's weird how quickly that happened – my entire life for almost a decade was focused on getting a TV series. I had gotten my dream series, with my dream production company, on my dream channel. And then it was gone, and I wasn't that upset about it. I had a new focus – I could come back to the other one if I survived long enough to. It all overlaps and gets jumbled in my mind, as it was all happening so fast that it's hard to keep the timeline straight, but it's essentially – out of hospital, *Beast Hunter* premiers, ACS/Stupid Cancer speeches start, ostomy is reversed, port-a-cath is installed, chemo starts, *Beast Hunter* is not renewed, we move to our first house, and chemo gets really bad and shuts my life down again. I'd also gone back to work in biotech in between the series premier and ACS speeches I think. They told me that I didn't need to and could stay on long-term disability through my six months of chemo, but to close on the house I couldn't be on medical leave, so I went back to work. I am a terrible patient.

Taking a step back, I recognize how stupid I was, and how I was pushing myself to go back to my old life. I hated the ostomy so much, but I basically just ignored it until it was time to change it or shower. I was putting off showering as much as possible and would go into a little depression in the hour before I knew I needed to change or do any maintenance on it. I had multiple homecare nurses coming every couple of days to help with all things ostomy-related, my incision wounds, and physical therapy. I was mostly leaving the house in Adidas trackpants and oversized sweatshirts so I could hide what was happening underneath. Once, however, someone asked to take a picture with me, and when they showed me the photo on their phone I noticed that you could see the ostomy bag sticking out from under my shirt. I deleted the picture and tried to play it off like I was making a weird face. The kind person didn't notice and was happy to take another picture with me – one where I made sure to hold my arms differently. It killed me a little inside. The bag also leaked a couple of times while I was out, which brought me to tears and made me start to give up on my future momentarily, but I kept reminding myself that it was temporary. I would likely only need the ostomy until the end of March, as the doctors wanted to remove it before I started chemo. When that date was confirmed, it was the best news I'd gotten since my diagnosis.

Going back to the hospital for yet another abdominal surgery gave me my first taste of so-called "white coat syndrome" – it's an involuntary reaction to seeing doctors that causes a mild panic attack. I still have it to this day. Even if I feel totally calm, my heart rate, blood pressure, and breathing will be off the charts. All of my doctors now know that they have to wait to take my vitals until the end of the visit, when I know I'm leaving. The anxiety this surgery produced was not subtle. I had a full-blown panic attack when they admitted me. It felt like I had just gotten out of the hospital and was now going back in – because that is exactly what was happening. I was only going to spend one night this time, though – maybe two. The procedure went well, I woke with my intestines back inside of me and a port-a-cath that looked like a doorbell installed under the skin on my left shoulder. (Anna would say "ding dong" and pretend to poke it once in a while.) This had a tube running directly to my heart, and would be where I'd receive chemo a couple weeks later.

The bag being gone was exciting and terrifying. I would wake in a cold sweat convinced that my intestines were going to flip and rupture again. Any stomach pain spelled immediate doom. It took me years to fully get over this feeling, and then only partially. On any given day, I can still be paralyzed by thoughts of my intestines rupturing again. I'm always just one stomach bug away from a major freak-out.

I was clearly pushing myself too hard, but I wanted my life back and I wanted it right then. I wanted to close on the house, to get back to filming, to be healthy – and in my mind, that meant being self-sufficient. I hated having people look after me, especially loved ones. When it was time to start chemo I insisted on taking a bus. I wouldn't accept any offer to drive me or sit with me or anything. I would take the bus, bring a book, have poison injected into me, get on the bus, and head home. I do not recommend this for anyone, nor do I recommend what I did later, which is drive myself to and from chemo.

I was going to get a dose of chemo every other Monday for about six months and I'd heard it wasn't going to get bad until about halfway through that regimen. That was incorrect. The chemo regime I would be getting involved going to the hospital, being hooked up through the port in my chest for about four hours, then having 20 hours' worth of medication placed in a fanny pack with a pump, continually injected into me via the needle/port in my chest, then having a homecare nurse come over to disconnect it, flush the line, and check on me the next day. This sounded straightforward, but involved an IT course on troubleshooting the pump and a lesson on "what can go wrong" with the home portion of the infusion. There was a protocol to follow if the needles came out of my port, another if the tubing from the fanny pack to the port got kinked while I was sleeping or vomiting, another if the bag of medication in the fanny pack ruptured, another if the pump malfunctioned, and another if I passed out. It was stressed to me, by multiple doctors and nurses, that under no circumstances was I or anyone else to touch the chemo drugs. If it leaked and went anywhere other than in my port, I was to put on a double pair of gloves and bag anything it touched in biohazard bags. If our pets ate it, they would die. If a person touched it, they would get very sick. My response to this was, "And this is being injected into my heart?"

The doctor looked at me and said, "Yes. This is poison. It is meant to kill human cells, and it does it very effectively. This is not 'medicine' in the traditional sense. It will do terrible things to you, but it will also save your life, we hope." And with that, I was ready to start.

My first chemo trip, I didn't know what to expect. I took the bus, got to the hospital, went to the oncology floor and met my chemo nurse, Sandy. She was one of the nicest, happiest people I have ever met – not happy as in bubbly, just with an inner peace radiating from her. She actually understood what I was going through and that I was going to be the quiet, "doing my own thing" patient, and she respected that. She didn't try to get me to join in the group talks (but did let me know they were available), didn't pressure me to have someone sit with me while I received the injection (but told me it was okay if I wanted it), and only talked to me when it seemed like I wanted to talk. She got me hooked up through my port for the first time and I was surprised that, although it was in my chest, I could "taste" the medication being injected. Sandy told me that about 20% of people had that unfortunate experience. The taste of the flush was nauseating – metallic and acrid. Not the best start. After the drugs were hooked up, I had four hours to kill. I read Jeremy Wade's forthcoming book and got lost in it for two hours, at which point a very nice volunteer brought around a snack tray.

I had some canned chicken noodle soup and a bag of plain potato chips. The second I tasted them I felt like I was going to vomit. The taste of food combined with the taste of the medication made my head spin. To this day, I can't eat either of those things without having a similar reaction. It's worse than any "I can't drink tequila after this one night in college" sensation. Even the thought of either of those foods makes me gag.

Walking still felt fairly new and exciting for me, so I decided to gather up my IV bags and tubes and walk around the floor. The first thing I noticed was that I was at least 20 years younger than the next youngest person there. The next was that I was only 1 of 2 people who didn't have someone with them, and the third thing was that the other person was a friend of mine. Michele Dionne, my boss from my first marine biology internship when I was 16, was sitting there, hooked up to an IV, getting her dose of chemo, and reading a book about wildlife. She had hired me and brought me to Maine to live by myself in a barn, and taught me to channel my love of wildlife into public outreach and education. She was a force for good in the world and a passionate conservationist. She inspired me more than I'd been able to express at 16, and here was my opportunity to tell her. I couldn't believe it. We spoke, and she said she'd read the *Boston Globe* article and was glad to hear I was still reaching people with a scientific message, and even happier that I was doing better health-wise. We talked for the remainder of the time, and it was really good to reconnect with her. We stayed in touch and received a few more doses of chemo together. A year later, unfortunately, she passed away at the age of 58. I wish her story could have ended differently, but cancer is a terrible disease that doesn't care what an amazing person you are, and as she would say, "In 1996 I was given 6 months to live, every day since has been a bonus and a gift." Chemo and other treatments had allowed her to see her kids grow, to see the conservation movement in America gain momentum, and to see the Wells reserve grow and blossom under her direction. She was a remarkable woman and the first of many "cancer friends" to pass away. It never gets easier.

Chatting with Michele made the time fly, and it was soon time to get back on the bus and head home. Aside from the nausea from the chicken soup/chips, I actually felt fine. It seemed like what I'd read was correct – this first dose wasn't terrible. I got my fanny pack cinched up around my waist, hid the tubes in my sweatshirt, bought some cookies in the hospital cafeteria, and hopped on the bus. I was warned about a possible side effect called neuropathy, an extreme sensitivity to cold where even room temperature items can feel like they've been soaked in liquid nitrogen. I was told that taking a sip of cold water would feel like drinking razors, and issued a warm hat, gloves, and socks, but they didn't seem necessary and remained in my backpack. After that first dose I was feeling good, and was thinking maybe I'd been unlucky enough to get to "taste" the medicine through the port, but had been spared the neuropathy and nausea – that seemed like a good trade! I also knew that all the effects of the chemo would intensify and last longer with each dose – like, the second dose would be worse than the first, the third worse than the second, etc.

I ate the cookies on the bus, read a bit more of Jeremy's book, and attempted to get as comfortable as I could with two needles in my chest and a fanny pack full of poison around my waist – poison that was being pumped into my heart. I was still feeling fine by the time I reached home.

When I'd found out I needed chemo, Adam had baked me some pot brownies. Being a science nerd, I had never smoked or eaten cannabis. He told me how much to eat and how long it would take to kick-in, etc. Adam has been my best friend since he was born. He's the son of my parents' best friends, and his older sister Laura was Sarah's age and her best friend. I was apparently at the hospital when Adam was born, but, being six months old, I don't remember the first time we met. He is basically my brother and we were together more often than not for the first 18 years of our lives. I'm pretty sure he didn't really like me until we were 10, but he put up with all of my weirdness on the unspoken rule that I'd play guns and ride bikes for about the same amount of time that he'd catch snakes and bugs and talk about obscure movies and bands. Adam always accepted me for who I was, and his love and support made me so much more comfortable in being the weirdo that I was.

We went on vacation together every year to Seabrook, New Hampshire. Why Seabrook? Weirdly, a lot of people from Upstate New York made Seabrook their vacation destination. My father's family had been going there since the 1950s, and he said that in the fifties it had a reputation for the most affordable oceanfront rentals within a couple of hundred miles. Seabrook is nice, sort of your stereotypical New England seaside town. But just over a drawbridge is Hampton. Hampton is a super cheesy boardwalk town that hit 1986 and decided, "I've peaked! This is it! I'm good," and has never left. I was there in 1986, when it was the most 1986 it could be, really living its best life. Airbrushed T-shirts everywhere, big hair, short-shorts on everyone. It was amazing, and still is today.

While we were there, Adam and I would pretend we were brothers from Hawaii to "impress girls". In all the years of working on these identities – long conversations into the night about the adventures we went on in Hawaii, how the surfing was so much better on "locals only beaches", how the moon looked over the water at sunset – and since, neither of us ever visited Hawaii, we weren't exactly sure if we were correct in our statements. Luckily, I think we only once told an actual girl this cover, and didn't go any deeper than, "Where are you guys here from?"

As I was too paralyzed with fear to actually speak, Adam replied, "Hawaii."

"Cooooooooool," said the random NH girl. "But not really right? Okay, later." Adam, being blonde, muscular, athletic, and very tan, could have pulled off this story alone, but with me next to him – with perpetually broken and taped glasses, being very overweight, and falling down a lot – no one was going to buy that we were brothers, much less surfer brothers from Hawaii.

Adam was in a band, Action Action, who were touring North America and playing with famous bands, getting played on MTV, etc., and he knew way more about weed than I did. I was thinking about the brownies in the fridge and how much I'd appreciated the gesture, but how it was unlikely I would need them based on that day. By about 8pm I'd wished I'd eaten a brownie.

It started when I went to the kitchen to have a glass of water. I was feeling fine, but took a sip and felt like my throat was being split open. I dropped the cup and started gagging. Anna ran to see what was happening, and I spluttered, "Neuropathy! Shit! Shit that hurts!" We both kind of laughed because the sensation was gone as quickly as it had come. "Great, this is not a good sign," I said as the nausea kicked in. It wasn't terrible, it was just like suddenly having a hangover. Not a really bad one, but it hitting me out of nowhere was disconcerting. I told Anna I was going to go to sleep and hopefully feel better in the morning. I had to sleep on my back because of the needles in my chest – and I am a stomach sleeper – so I lay awake in bed feeling like shit for a couple of hours before finally drifting off. This had become my routine as I couldn't sleep on my stomach in the hospital or after, and I never got used to sleeping on my back.

I woke up feeling like shit, barely able to get out of bed, but after the nurse came over and unhooked the IV I started feeling better. By that evening I felt as good as I had before chemo, and surprised everyone at work by coming in the next day. My good friend Bill – my boss at the time who then transitioned to mentor, who I now trade recipes and brewing tips with, and whose son was the planner for our surprise wedding – was definitely not expecting to see me.

"Pat! What are you doing here? Didn't you have chemo a

couple days ago? You know you don't need to come in? We have you only working every other week, and I think even that's pushing it." Bill, and the company I worked for at the time, were amazing, if you can't tell. I had worked there for 10 years and seen it quadruple in size from a small biotech to one of the largest in the area. They were beyond good to me – it still shocks people when I say that my entire cancer experience, from diagnosis to completing chemo, including multiple ambulance rides, homecare nurses, PT, and dozens of prescriptions, cost me about $250 out of pocket. It's unreal, and I'm so fortunate to be able to say that. From the moment I said, "I have cancer," Bill assured me that I would be able to "work whenever I was physically and mentally able," with zero concern for my employment status. It was something I later found out was far from normal, and am still immensely grateful for.

"I know, and I appreciate it, but I genuinely feel fine. That might not be the case down the road, so I'd rather work now while I can." After a bit more convincing that I was okay, they let me stay.

Two weeks later I was heading back in to see Sandy and spend another couple of hours talking to Michele. The bus ride back was uneventful, but the neuropathy and nausea kicked in a few hours earlier than they had with dose one, and were much worse. This time it was like a bad hangover, and the bottoms of my feet hurt just walking on the floor without socks. I didn't need the wooly hat and scarves, but could see that was the direction this was going in. Three days later, I was okay and back to work again.

The third dose of chemo was on my 31st birthday. Anna and I had moved into our new house the day before, and I now lived over an hour from the hospital and not on a bus route, so I planned to drive myself. The side effects at that point weren't kicking in until late in the evening, so I figured I was fine and safe. My doctors didn't love the idea, but they also thought that any sense of freedom I felt was good for me, so they didn't say a lot. I had to drive by Dunkin' Donuts and a Boston Market, and started a tradition of stuffing my face before the nausea kicked in.

So, there I was, turning 31, trying to force myself to focus on something other than the metallic taste in my mouth and cloudy feeling in my head. I stared with the CNN homepage on my phone, and learned that Bin Laden had been killed early that morning in a country far away. I wanted, very badly, to be in a country far away – not necessarily the same country as Bin Laden and SEAL Team Six, but on some adventure, and certainly not in a hospital in Boston. For that day, though, my only traveling was back to my new house. If you had asked me the year before how I thought I'd be spending my 31st birthday, I don't think the reality could have possibly been further from what my answer would have been.

After getting home, anticipating the onset of the side effects, and as a birthday gift to myself, I ate my first pot brownie. I measured it, with a tape measure, and ate exactly two square inches. The first time I had ever had cannabis. The nausea came, but not nearly as bad – and I had already eaten a bag of M&Ms, some Doritos, a pizza, and some cookies, so may not have even been chemo related. I just want to say that cannabis is amazing! What a great discovery. I called Adam and thanked him, for about an hour, and then went to sleep.

I woke up feeling like shit, and this continued until well after the IV was removed. The neuropathy was getting to be a concern as well. The doctors said it was progressing faster than they'd expected – I was having symptoms on my third dose that most people don't develop until their 8th or 9th dose. Neuropathy can become permanent, and the doctors were tracking its progress and weighing it against the benefits of the combo of drugs I was getting. I was scared, because removing one of the drugs would lessen the effects of the neuropathy, but would also potentially reduce the efficacy of the treatment. I asked to stick it out for at least a few more doses.

By the fourth dose I was wearing wooly socks, a scarf, fleece sweatpants, a sweatshirt, a fanny pack, and a winter hat – in mid-May. My feet felt like pins and needles for 3-4 days, I couldn't drink or even touch cold water for a week, and I was almost out of brownies – which I was no longer sizing with a tape measure. This had all escalated quickly. One of my new neighbors stopped by the house to say hello, and I shuffled to the door looking like I was ready to go sledding in a blizzard despite it being a beautiful and warm spring day, then realized how crazy I must appear and started to ramble about chemo. I was also high. Welcome to the neighborhood! Coincidently, he was a doctor, and at least pretended to totally understand.

I asked my oncologist if they could prescribe cannabis, and told him that it was the only thing that seemed to help with the nausea, insomnia, anxiety, pain, and appetite. It really is a wonder drug. He told me that in Massachusetts he couldn't, but, in his own words, "You're 31, Pat. I'm sure you have some friends who can help you out here." And he was right!

Anna and I are both science nerds. Anna had smoked weed once and eaten one pot brownie before I got cancer. Neither of us had ever bought it, nor given much thought to it. One of our friends knew a lot about it, especially the economics of it – wink-wink, nudge-nudge. What I'm trying to say is he was a drug dealer. We actually had a lot of friends who were drug dealers – you can't really come up in the punk scene and not – but one said he would give us as much of the best weed as we wanted at cost. I was home, curled up in the fetal position on the couch, so Anna took $100 and went to buy an ounce. I assumed that would be about 2-3 joints. It turned out to be significantly more than that. Anna walked in the house with a large baggie. We both started laughing at our own ignorance, and then I realized that I needed to learn how to smoke.

When I was 12, my sister and I rolled lemon zinger tea in coffee filters and smoked it, something my mom had done in high school and we thought sounded fun. When she and my father found out, instead of getting angry, they laughed and then showed us how to roll a really good "tea cigarette". My mom was pregnant with my little brother at the time, and wasn't exactly thinking straight.

I'd fallen out of practice since then, and the joint I tried to roll was not working. For one thing, apparently you need to break up the weed, and not just put a whole bud in the rolling paper. I was back on the phone with Adam, who could not stop laughing at me.

"Wait, wait – you just put a whole bud in the rolling paper? HAHAHAHHA! Jesus, Patrick, that's amazing."

"I didn't even know it was a bud. I called it a 'clump'. Yeah, I don't know what I'm doing."

"Clearly. Okay, give up on joints. Get a bowl."

"A bowl…?"

"A glass pipe with a little bowl-shaped thing on one end."

"Ah! Okay, yeah, I know what that is. Where do I buy one?"

"Is there a sketchy gas station near you?"

Donning my finest giant old skater hoodie, fleece sweatpants, wooly hat, and snow-boot ensemble (it was 70 degrees out), I drove to New Hampshire to the sketchiest gas station/ convenience store combo I could think of.

"Hello! Do you sell 'bowls' here," I said to the angry-looking old man behind the bulletproof glass at the counter, who was as confused as I was why I'd made air-quotes when I said "bowls". I wanted to look less conspicuous, so I was also buying some Doritos, a bag of circus peanuts, a 6-pack of Coors Light, and a bottle of lime juice. "Nothing shady going on here," my purchases said in my addled brain. "Just a normal day of shopping."

"Balls?" he asked.

"No, sorry. Bowls. Like, glass bowls, for, um, for smoking, you know," and I mimed what I thought smoking from a bowl would look like.

Clearly and justifiably disgusted, he said, "We have glass pipes to smoke tobacco with. Is that what you want?"

"No, I don't smoke tobacco."

"Then I don't think I can help you," said the clearly frustrated old man. "You have to sign a form that you will use these to smoke tobacco from in order for me to sell you one."

"OH! ... Tobacco! ... Yes, I would like to buy a bowl to smoke tobacco from. Thank you!"

I signed the form, thanked the man, and bought a green one for $15. Back at home and on the phone with Adam I said: "Okay, I broke up the pot with my fingers and put as much in the bowl as I could. Now, do I light the bottom? Like, heat up the glass?"

"Oh. My. God. I wish I was there. No, Patrick, It's not crack. HAHAHHAHA. Holy shit. No, you light the actual weed, then cover the air intake, then..." And this way, slowly and patiently, Adam taught me how to smoke weed.

The doctors had me on a dozen different drugs, from lorazepam to experimental antinausea, and none of them worked as well as weed. I wasn't able to go into work until Thursday or Friday on the weeks I received treatment by that point, so Anna never knew what she was going to come home to after work. Some evenings I'd be curled up on the floor of some room in our house, wherever I was when the nausea, dizziness, or anxiety hit really badly, unable to move or speak for a few hours, or maybe even a day. Other times I'd be baking cookies and leaving the oven on. Maybe I'd be in a pool of vomit. Maybe catatonic on the couch. Twice I was outside on a hill behind our house laying in the grass and staring at the stars. When Anna asked me how long I'd been out there, I just said, "Since I left the house," and, "Isn't it beautiful?" Anna started getting worried about these activities and my safety, so decided we'd find some good TV for the two of us to get into.

After getting home from chemo (still driving myself, even though the side effects were coming faster now so it was sort of a race against the clock), Anna had the TV prepped with a series neither of us had watched when it initially aired – *Lost*. I went behind our house, smoked a lot of weed, then came in ready for some TV binging. Five hours later, Anna was ready to call it a night. I said I was going to stay up and watch a couple more. When she woke up the next day, I was still on the couch.

"Hey, you're up early, what did I miss?"

"Season 2. I'm not going to be able to catch you up, sorry."

I proceeded to watch the entire *series* of *Lost* in four straight days. I was not disappointed in the ending. I think I cried. I was, however, smoking a lot of weed and not sleeping.

Chemo never seemed to end. It had reached the point where I had more bad days than good, and for the last two doses I finally relented and admitted I couldn't drive myself, but I also wasn't going to need anyone to drive me, because I wasn't going to get the last two doses. I had decided to end chemo early. My doctors and I talked about it very seriously, and I had made up my mind that it didn't matter anymore. It had gotten so bad, and had lasted so long, that I just wanted it to be over. I felt terrible all the time. I had developed severe acne for the first time in my life, my teeth were shot – I had never had a cavity before, and now I was looking at 10 of them and tooth sensitivity for the rest of my life. Everything hurt. My hair was thinning. My stomach looked like Frankenstein's monster, missing a bellybutton, scars covering the rest of it. I couldn't touch anything colder than my own body temperature, and I hadn't been able to feel my feet for over a month. The doctors had cut one of the drugs out a few doses before because the neuropathy had gotten so bad, but the feeling hadn't come back and they didn't know if it ever would. But I was still "working" when I could. I would show up, anyway, but chemo brain is real and I was useless. I was still giving speeches and attempting to relaunch *Nature Calls*, getting one of my best friends and the co-producer Dom to come over and film snakes with me in my backyard whenever I convinced myself I was well enough. The footage was all terrible. In reality, it was Anna and Dom humoring me, helping me do something I loved to get my mind off of what was happening to my body and life.

My parents and Anna were very concerned about my ending chemo early, not finishing the full regimen as recommended by the doctors. But Anna, who was with me every day, was also very concerned with what it was doing to me and who I would be by the end of it all. I was miserable and looked like death most days towards the end. And "the end" was theoretically in sight, but not for me. Two more doses seemed like an eternity and I couldn't bring myself to face it. I was so close, but it seemed a bridge too far. After a very long conversation with my parents, whom I had called to tell of my decision, I reversed course and decided to finish the treatments.

My father is the reason I moved to Boston for college. I was deciding between two schools which were giving me almost full tuition – one in a small town, and Suffolk University in Boston. Al told me how challenging Boston would be, and how much more comfortable he knew I was with the campus in a small town, but how challenges shaped who we are and what amazing opportunities cities had to offer as opposed to campuses in small towns. Suffolk had no campus – it's on Beacon Hill, and the buildings are scattered around the statehouse. We talked for a long time, and I thought about it all night, then chose Suffolk in the morning. He seemed happy, if a little surprised, and completely supported my decision, and talked me through sticking it out when the first semester was challenging. Years later, after I'd graduated, I told him how much that conversation had meant to me and how right he was. He replied, "Well, clearly I was wrong. I was trying to convince you NOT to go to Boston, saying how much more comfortable you'd be at the other school." I had heard him, but taken the opposite message of, "Challenge yourself, now is the time to do it, step out of your comfort zone, I know you can do anything you can set your mind to, etc." What really resonated in regards to chemo was him saying that there were a million reasons to stop. But there are always a million reasons to not do something, I needed to find the reason to keep going. I needed to make that decision and challenge myself again. I needed to actively commit to staying alive, right then, as hard as that was and for whatever reason. I needed to, at the bare minimum, decide that I wanted to live.

In September I received my last dose of chemo; I had made it through all of them. I asked Anna's cousin to drive me to the last couple of treatments, and that – asking for help – was one of the hardest things for me to do. As an adult, I had only ever asked someone for help before cancer once. I asked my sister if I could borrow $225 once when Anna and I were really broke and we weren't going to be able to pay rent because my crappy car had broken down, our budget had absolutely no wiggle room, and I had already sold anything of value that I felt we could part with. She sent me a check for $1,000 immediately and never mentioned it again, aside from telling me that of course I couldn't pay it back, when I tried a few months later. Other than that, it wasn't until those last two doses of chemo that I realized that asking people for help was okay. I was glad to help when a loved one asked. Likewise, they would be glad to help. It was hard to wrap my head around, though. I've heard similar sentiments from other cancer survivors – for me it was not wanting to feel like a burden. Ten years on, I have gotten much more okay with it, and I don't drive myself to follow-up scans, colonoscopies, or surgeries. My father-in-law Carl is generally tapped to transport a very drugged-up me from these appointments, and he has now gained some fun anecdotes about the things a person says when they are coming down from massive amounts of painkillers and anesthesia.

Sandy had a little party for me in the oncology ward after the last dose. Michele had finished her round of chemo a few weeks before, but sent me a nice e-mail commemorating the occasion. I felt awful for the next three weeks, despite the weed, lorazepam, and a bunch of other drugs. Then slightly less awful, then not terrible, then okay. It was about six months before I felt sort of normal – or at least my new baseline for normal – and closer to a year before I felt like myself, and over a year before I regained the feeling in one of my feet. I was sitting on the couch one night with Anna and out of nowhere said, "HOLY SHIT! I can feel my foot! And it REALLY hurts!" Apparently, I had broken my toe at some point, and known nothing about it. So physically I went back to normal-ish, but mentally I was a mess. There would be about 15 minutes every day when I would be absolutely crippled by the thought that the cancer had come back. I mean, paralyzed – unable to move or speak because I was so convinced.

A normal thought would go like this: "My armpit kind of hurts. It must be cancer. It can't be the curls I did yesterday at the gym, it's cancer. How could I get cancer in my armpits? Can deodorant give you cancer? [Google search.] SHIT! I knew it! I have cancer in my armpits from my deodorant! Should I stop wearing deodorant? ANNA! Should I stop wearing deodorant? I think I have cancer from it..."

Anna did not think I should stop wearing deodorant, or that my headache or the pain in my side was cancer. She didn't even think it was cancer when I got a weird result back from one of the dozens of tests the doctors were running on me every couple of months. She was always reassuring me that I was okay. I had read that the most likely place for colon cancer that had metastasized to show up was as bladder cancer, so, unfortunately for Anna, we talked about my pee a lot, and more unfortunately she was called into the bathroom to look at my pee on a few occasions.

I had to believe that it was okay to be okay before I could move past this. I had anxiety, for sure, but I also had survivor's guilt. It took me a long time. Ativan helped a bit, but also made me really sleepy, and after the morphine experience I didn't want to take any prescription meds. The anxiety was really bad over the winter, especially because there wasn't anything else to occupy my mind. I'd spent eight+ years entirely focused on TV, and a little over a year focused on surviving, and now I had decided I really wanted to live, but was basically living in fear in between every medical visit. Each month I would have a weird blood result, or an odd scan, or an unexplained pain. It got to be a little too much, and once again Anna encouraged me to throw myself back into something more productive than googling bladder-cancer symptoms. I chose cancer speeches, and a real relaunch of *Nature Calls* – not just the terrible snake videos from my backyard, but a destination shoot.

Chapter 7

"If Driving 36 Hours Each Way to Lie Down in the World's Largest Pit of Snakes Doesn't Sound Like Fun to You, Then I Don't Know If We Can Be Friends"

By the time my birthday rolled around again, I was ready for an adventure. I was not quite fit enough to take out an international terrorist the way SEAL Team Six had done the previous year, but I was definitely ready to catch some snakes.

Dom was also ready. He and I had filmed a few episodes while I was doing chemo, but we both knew it wasn't the same. I was off, I was slow, and we couldn't really do anything too outrageous or travel too far from my doctor. Every time I stumbled over my words or didn't catch the animal we had been going for, Dom would make fun of me, just like normal. He knew I was sick, but didn't treat me like it. He knew I couldn't feel my feet and had cold sensitivity in my hands, but also that I was trying to ignore these and, following my lead, did the same. By treating me like he normally would he helped me feel like I was normal, and I'll always be grateful for that. He, Anna, and Adam also started my ongoing, groan-inducing, love of cancer-humor. One of my favorites was to tell people, "One of the best things about beating cancer is that I don't need to wear sunblock anymore," and the person would confusedly ask, "Why?" "I've already had it right? It's like chickenpox," then watch their reactions. I loved using this line in front of Dom because even though he knew it was coming – he'd always genuinely groan and laugh while the other person got very uncomfortable and wondered if they needed to break some news to me, or if they should laugh.

Dom had some good ones himself. He would say, "Think about all of the things you've done! You got a TV show on National Geographic! You did the bullet ant ritual! You beat cancer!", then add, "At least, until right now." When I got bitten by a snake because my reflexes were off, Dom didn't ask how I was. Instead, he just said, "That poor snake. It has no idea the shit that's in your blood right now. You probably just poisoned it."

I needed to do something for my 32nd birthday that would prove to myself more than anyone else that I was back, that I was healthy, and that I could do all of the things I had done before cancer. Anna and I were still unpacking the house, I had started a new day job that was a slightly shorter drive from our new place, and we were starting to plan what would turn into our surprise wedding. It's a slight understatement to say our budget was tight and we didn't have too much free time, but that had never stopped us before. I called Dom in March and asked him if he'd ever heard of the Manitoba snake dens. His response was, "Of *course* I have! Who do you think you're talking to? When are we going? Jarrod will come as second camera," and thus our next trip was born – we would be driving over 2,000 miles to Manitoba, Canada to find the largest concentration of snakes on Earth, and lay down in the middle of them – something I had wanted to do since I was a little kid.

In very typical *Nature Calls* fashion (we eventually sold the footage to the BBC for an episode of *Nature's Weirdest Events* but it was a *Nature Calls* shoot), we had an extremely tight window to film in, next to no budget, and were doing all of the planning ourselves – by which I mean *I* was doing all of the planning. I contacted the Department of Conservation in Manitoba, explained who we were, what we were looking to do, and asked for some advice regarding how to pull this off. I've learned that it's always good to lead with, "I'm a presenter for the National Geographic Channel," before getting into, "I want to lay down in a pit of snakes and put the video on the interwebs." Canadians being Canadian, they were super nice and helpful, and said "eh" a lot.

Fortunately for us, the filming and temporary permit fees turned out to be minimal. After seeing some *Nature Calls* videos, a very kind government representative even offered to allow us to camp out near the snakes to save money on a hotel. He told us that my birthday fell right around the predicted prime snake-emergence, but with the weather as the main factor in the presence or absence of snakes on any given day, we couldn't be guaranteed to see much of anything, and our best bet was to plan on being there about a week, minimum, in order to have a good chance of one really nice, warm, sunny day. This kind of weather would lead to the maximum number of snakes above ground mating. Oh, did I mention that's what the snakes are doing? That it's actually a massive snake orgy that we were planning on laying down in the middle of? No? Okay, more on that later, then.

We didn't have a week, and we didn't have the $2,200 each for plane tickets – what we did have was my aging Scion xB car and a whole lot of free food due to a photography job Dom had recently done where he was paid in produce – not an entirely uncommon or unwelcome event in his career. Dom has proposed a few novel payment methods over the years, including: "a box of donuts every other day for two years"; "all the booze I can physically carry from behind your bar"; "eight hours to do anything I want with that cobra"; and "a megaphone", two of which he received, much to the excitement/dismay of *many* of his close friends.

Dom is one of my best friends. He's also one of the most talented, driven, unique, and difficult-to-describe people I've ever met. He's an obscenely talented photographer, videographer, and sculptor who has won Best of Boston awards and been published in numerous international magazines, and

– much like Ben, the director of the Canada and Brazil episodes of *Beast Hunter* – is always working and trying to make it seem like he isn't. It's a rare moment when Dom and I are not collaborating on, or at least planning, a project. It's what we both do – we absolutely love thinking up new ideas and making them happen. We live it, every day. It never feels like work when we are at a bar on a Friday night with our notebooks out, planning our next adventure.

Dom is the consummate artist. I can't picture him not creating something or pushing himself towards his next goal. All of his varied living situations have been surreal walk-in art experiences. They've featured teepees, speakeasys, self-stuffed animals, antiques, self-tanned animal hides, and, currently, a bed made from birch trees felled by beavers in his backyard and a fence stolen from my backyard under the cover of night. In this and many other ways, Dom literally lives art; but, because it's so engrained in his everyday life, he doesn't realize how remarkable his work is. To him, it's just his life. Like all great artists, he is never satisfied and never finished, which can be tough on those around him who want to see him happy. This sounds wrong – he *is* happy, he's one of the few people I know who really enjoys life, but he's rarely proud of any of the amazing work he's produced, and even the most outrageous and impressive things he does quickly fade into the background, replaced by the next once-in-a-lifetime experience or trip that, for nearly everyone else in the world, would be their defining moment – brought up at dinner parties, college essays, or in their obituaries – while for Dom it's a Tuesday.

Trying to describe Dom is challenging – do I describe him as he is today? The thoughtful, self-aware artist who would rather spend a week in the woods with his amazing wife and son than a week documenting the orgies and bacchanalia that is Bonnaroo? Or do I describe the Dom of his early twenties, when he was living and breathing chaos? A man whose 22nd birthday ended with a literal flood of beer despite not having a drop himself (honestly, beer two inches deep covering the floor of a Mission Hill apartment) and a naked pudding-wrestling match between himself and four young women in the kitchen? A man who would walk into Walmart to buy some bacon and end up playing a rousing game of soccer in the aisles? A man whose MySpace page wasn't checked or updated since the day it was created, and featured a photo of himself wearing a loincloth and covered head to toe in blood, dancing in front of a bonfire made from smashed furniture in some sort of tribal rite of passage, and looking every bit the pagan god of destruction?

No, it seems wrong and unfair to describe him as such, partially because his thirties self would laugh and shake his head at that person if they met today, but mostly because that was only ever one small part of Dom. It was just such a loud, absurd, amazing, and engrossing part that it was all most people saw. Like a moth to a flame, everyone who saw this aspect of Dom's nature was drawn to him. Everyone was waiting to see what would happen next, and Dom *never* disappointed, and still doesn't. It would be inaccurate to say it was an act, or performance art – it absolutely was not. It was definitely Dom being himself, but it wasn't 24/7 as you might think after hanging out with him for a short time during one of these impromptu excursions. It also wasn't for anyone other than himself, his own amusement, which was also hard to see at first. It was easy to mistake as an act, a put on, for a rapt audience. But the more time you spent with Dom, the more you realized he would be doing this whether you were there or not.

I consider myself extremely fortunate to know the other side of Dom – the Dom behind the hedonistic Dom, even in those early days. I think few people can say this – Dom has a huge group of friends, many of whom have become my close friends as well, but in the group I think there are a select few of us, a sort of inner circle, who have gotten to know Dom as a whole person, and all of our lives are richer for it. The above Dom disappeared for all intents and purposes after one of his bike trips across the country. With no planning or preparation, he pedaled a bicycle coast to coast, twice. After the first one he came back calmer, more Zen-like in everyday life, saving the partying for appropriate times and then unleashing his inner Jello-wrestler when he was most needed. He also contracted scurvy. Maybe that had something to do with it. Maybe getting a pirate disease which is literally cured with orange juice made him realize that he needed a slight lifestyle change. Probably not, though. I've never known Dom to change based on anything other than his own whims. After the bike trip, and of course the subsequent scurvy, Dom seemed able to channel his energy into being more productive and focused. He started taking on fewer projects and focused entirely on photography, *Nature Calls*, and sculpture.

Describing him physically is just as problematic. When I met Dom he had massive dreads that sprang into existence after not washing his hair for a few months while simultaneously spending each day of the spring, summer, and fall swimming in a different body of water – oceans, lakes, glorified puddles, ponds, abandoned pools, streams, swimming holes, quarries. Basically, any water New England has to offer. Various young ladies had woven trinkets and reminders of themselves and their fleeting time in Dom's life into these dreads. He couldn't remember much about any of them. He wore giant bug-eye sunglasses all the time, no shirt, and a pair of rolled-up camo-cargo pants which had honestly never been washed. You might have thought he was a hippy at first glance, until you found out he didn't drink or smoke, ate an astonishing amount of meat (which, along with pancakes, made up more than 90% of his diet), and was one of the most inappropriate people you could come across. He seemed like Nick Offerman's teenage self or a caricature of a rebellious former-hippy-turned-yuppie's kid.

After getting sick of being known as "the guy with dreads", he shaved his head and traded the bug-eyes for multicolored Ray-Bans. The head shaving occurred in a dugout canoe he had built himself after spending some time with the local Wampanoag Native American tribe to learn the skill. This way, he was able to introduce his freshly-shorn scalp to lake water immediately, and swim to shore renewed – but that's a story for another time. After volunteering to tear down houses in a post-Katrina New Orleans, he had to burn the camo-cargos because they were quite literally classified as "biohazardous waste" by a physician, who determined they were harboring black mold and other toxins that were making Dom and his companions on the road trip very sick.

He will occasionally show up sporting a massive woodsman's beard, which seems to grow in about a fortnight, alternates between pink flip-flops, cowboy boots, and bare feet, with white faux-fur coats or V-necks in a seasonally appropriate manner, and has theme outfits such as "red" or "denim", in which he covers himself head to toe. The days of him showing up in speedos to go out for ice cream may be over, but you still really never know what Dom is going to look like from day to day. He is consistently tall, thin, and lithe, and walks with comfort, seeming to glide with ease into and out of every situation. Even when viewed from a distance, you can tell an artist is approaching.

All of this aside, the main reason Dom was on this trip with me was because of his kindness and generosity. Dom's time is the most valuable thing to him, and it's one of the things he is able to be generous with. He budgets his time the way most people do their finances, and only spends it on the things which are most important to him. He may not remember birthdays or Christmas, but, when you need him, Dom is always there for his friends. Whether it's tearing down an old shed, painting a couple of rooms, building a treehouse for your kids, or spending two days looking for a loose alligator in Rhode Island, Dom will be there. You can also count on him to make you amazing handmade gifts and postcards – sometimes showing up to family functions with ducks he just shot, maple syrup he spent a week collecting and boiling, or museum-quality framed photos that he's cut and mounted himself.

Dom was there with me through my chemo experience. He would come over and just sit on the couch and rewatch *Medicine Man* over and over, or talk, or help cook, or wake me up out of my daze and get me outside. Filming a bit, even as terrible as I was on camera, made me feel like myself – it felt like a part of me that had been neglected for over a year, and I loved getting back into it.

The day we were set to leave for the trip, Dom and his housemate Jarrod had a job in the morning that they couldn't turn down – they had just started their photography collective Little Outdoor Giants. We had been planning to leave in the early hours of the morning, but now had to shoot for a "sometime after dinner" target, so I went to my own day job that morning. After work, I drove the two hours back to my house, loaded up the car, said goodbye to Anna who had opted to not spend four days in a confined space with three dudes reeking of snake musk, and drove an hour and a half to Dom and Jarrod's place. Once there, it was clear we were not leaving anytime soon.

Jarrod was packing and Dom was nowhere to be seen. His car had died that afternoon and we'd need to push start it and get it to a shop on the way out of town. This unexpected delay had also pushed Dom's packing back a bit. This was all completely in line with every *Nature Calls* shoot to date. Jarrod and I hung out for a while until Dom arrived, disheveled, and scrambled to gather lenses, chargers, GoPros, hard drives, and, almost as an afterthought, a change of clothes. At about 11:30pm we left Dom's dead car parked outside of his uncle's auto body shop with a note and the keys, and we were off. Not a great start to the trip, but not the worst we'd ever had. On our first big international shoot in Costa Rica, I realized as we were boarding the plane that I had booked the non-refundable, non-exchangeable tickets for the wrong dates and we were going to have one less day to film than we had planned.

We were planning on driving nonstop the whole 36 hours to Manitoba and, despite having been awake since 7am, I volunteered to take the first shift. Dom had already been awake about 22 hours and was fighting off a cold. He generally eschews all medicine that isn't 100% necessary, so Jarrod and I were both shocked when he produced a bottle of Nyquil and asked if he could take the third shift. Intrigued, we both agreed. Dom smiled, said, "See you in 10 hours!", gulped three big swigs, and almost immediately passed out across the gear-covered backseat.

Jarrod and I spent the first few hours joking around, talking about what we'd been up to, determining a musical playlist for the next four days, and discussing the logistics of the shoot. We were planning to save money by taking up the Canadian Government's offer and camping out in a park that contained the snake dens. We also had enough peanut butter and jellies, cookies, chips, fruits and veggies, and junky camp food to last us the duration. Neither of us really knew what to expect. The weather was looking unpredictable and we wouldn't have any time to scout the location and determine the best way to film it – basically, we were showing up and hoping for the best. Again, all typical for a *Nature Calls* shoot.

By about 2am, Jarrod's eyes were drooping and I insisted I'd be fine and he should take a nap as he was next in line to drive. I had chugged an American-sized coffee at the last gas station and figured my heart palpitations alone would keep us from careening into oncoming traffic. The next five hours were the first time I was able to start processing what had happened to me in the past year. It had been simultaneously the best and worst year of my life. The pre-cancer plan had been a wrap filming *Beast Hunter* in late November, fun stuff with Anna, travel, house, etc, kick off a press tour with a promotional appearance at a massive TV conference in LA (the "upfront" for industry folks), then back to Boston for the holidays, and back out on the road for January and all of February for a series of interviews, speeches, and appearances, leading up to the show's premiere on March 11th. I'd at least made it to LA before everything went to shit.

The Upfronts were ridiculous and incredibly fun. The series producer Barny and the absolutely remarkable in every way Laura Marshall from Icon joined me. Laura always looks like she's just stepped out of a glamorous film noir, and has all of the social grace to match. She successfully guided me through the world of celebrity appearances, teaching me the social niceties and who's-who in the world of wildlife film and TV in general. We had drinks one night at the hotel bar and I found myself sipping a stupidly expensive Scotch next to a Kardashian. I didn't know who she was. Laura was fairly confident she was from a "horrible American reality show", but loved her dress and shoes. I had to text Anna and my sister and describe her to figure out her identity.

"She's very, very small, like tiny, and doesn't really look human. She's very pretty, but looks like a miniature perfect mannequin with huge, staring eyes, like she was assembled rather than being a living person, and Laura says her shoes are very expensive. Like a very short living doll. Group consensus is that she might be a Kardashian. Is there a Karly Kardashian? No? Karrie? No? She's not the one with the tape; I know that one. It's not important how I know. Okay, yes, she's very small. I'd guess three feet tall. Yes that might be an exaggeration. Okay, Kourtney, yes – that's her then, I think."

We didn't spend much time on the Kardashians or trying for sightings of Mike Tyson, Oprah, or Daniel Tosh, who were all promoting series as well. Instead, we stuck with the Nat Geo crew of Shawn Heflick, Brady Barr, and Henry Rollins. Shawn and Brady were hysterical, and we swapped war stories from various shoots – Brady won with an unidentified parasite still claiming residence in his scalp. I was definitely awed to be around these guys, especially Brady, who I had watched for years as he caught some of my favorite reptiles, but was a total fanboy around Henry Rollins. I knew he was going to be there promoting his *Snake Underground* special, and I had brought a vinyl copy of Black Flag's *Damaged* for him to sign. Turned out he had seen the promotional episode of *Beast Hunter* and really liked it! We talked music a little, but mostly shared travel stories. Henry has been all over the world doing various humanitarian work, and was passionate about the cause of equal rights for all. I was practically attached to his hip the whole weekend, and he was incredibly nice to me. He was very down to Earth, introverted, polite, kind, and remarkably humble. Months later, my father sent him an original 12x18 print of a brilliant photo he'd taken inside the seminal punk venue CBGBs weeks before it closed. The picture has earned some well-deserved accolades from various aficionados and gormandizers, and a copy currently hangs in the John Varvatos shop where CBs once stood. Henry sent back a very thoughtful, personal note to my father and me about how special CBGBs was to him, and how much he liked the print. It meant a lot coming from a guy like Hank.

I returned from LA and started mentally preparing myself to launch my new life as "Pat Spain, Wildlife TV Host". I was in the best shape of my life physically (I thought) and was literally living my wildest dreams, working for Icon Films and Nat Geo, and planning future travels. I described it to my friends by saying: "Imagine the Red Sox asked you to become their general manager." I had made some incredible new friends at Icon, Anna and I were looking to buy our first house, and I was finally getting out of the massive debt that *Nature Calls* had put me in. At one point, in late fall, Anna and I were on our way to Logan and I turned to her and asked if she was ready for all of this: "I know we've talked about it a lot, but it looks like life as we know is changing; massively. I want to make sure you're okay with this. There will be some challenges in scheduling, we may have to move holidays to other dates, miss family and friends' events, and be a lot more mobile. I just want to make sure that this is what you want." She said of course it was. In fact, she couldn't wait to see what the future held for us. A new life was just starting.

All of that changed with my cancer diagnosis in January. I went from the highest point of my life to the lowest in a matter of weeks. Suddenly, rather than moving forward at breakneck pace, every aspect of our life was on hold. This trip to Canada to experience the snake dens would be my symbolic return. Sure, I wasn't the same guy I'd been on *Beast Hunter* – I hoped I'd be better. I was certainly more wrinkled and grey, which all the networks seemed to love. I was back, driving to Manitoba in a car full of gear with two of my incredible friends at 7am after not sleeping for 24 hours, heading into the unknown. We were doing this and nothing would stop us – not cancer, not finances, not day jobs, not even sleep. Well, maybe sleep.

I started to have little microsleeps behind the wheel around Buffalo, New York, and when I started actually hallucinating I figured it was time to wake Jarrod. I saw a giant neon cowboy chasing a rabbit on the side of the road and thought, "Cancer didn't kill me, but driving right now might." I pulled over to get gas and we all switched positions. A groggy Jarrod jumped behind the wheel, and we gave up on waking up Dom so I slept like a rock in the passenger seat, content in the knowledge that I had made all of the right decisions regarding this expedition.

I woke a couple hours outside of Chicago. We decided to stop and get some deep-dish and started texting everyone we knew who had ever lived there for advice on the best, eventually deciding on Lou Malnati's after inciting some particularly aggressive arguments. Dom had come back to life somewhere before Toledo and it seemed like he'd hibernated through whatever ailment he needed to fight off. We stopped, peed, grabbed the pizza to go, had some lit cigarettes thrown at us from a moving car (love you, Chicago!), jumped back in our now-starting-to-smell-like-a-road-trip car, and fought rush-hour traffic to leave the city.

It was a few hours before we were hungry again, and we were just getting into Wisconsin as the sun went down. Jarrod said we needed more cheese curd in our life, and he wasn't wrong. Regional foods are some of the best parts of road trips. Once, outside of Tucson, Arizona, at an unsavory-looking gas station, I purchased handfuls of "candy", which is how it was labeled, with cartoon drawings of happy children. One of the packets was dried whole jumbo shrimp, another was a very gummy, odd-flavored, fruit strip coated in super-hot chili pepper, and another was just straight-up jalapenos. The curd was much better than any of these.

The weather turned ugly soon after with freezing rain, just as I was set to take my next turn behind the wheel. I drove for a couple hours, white knuckled behind the wheel of my notoriously unstable car, until I saw signs for the border crossing a little after 2am. This line was not just where we would be transported in the world of "eh's" and "oo's", but also where my GPS would give out and we would be transported back to 2005 with paper directions printed from MapQuest. I woke the guys to prepare.

Dom, who has flown internationally with me before, immediately told me to pull over and let him drive. Jarrod was confused until Dom explained my complete ineptitude at dealing with, and irrational fear of, border police. All police, actually. I have a problem with playing it cool. Even if I'm not doing anything wrong. I get very nervous and jumpy and start acting like a terrified drug mule or arms dealer before they even ask their first question. My close friends know this, and it doesn't help when they shout to various TSA officials, "He has drugs up his ass!" as they happily walk through to the gate. If I see a cop on the side of the highway, I'm the guy who slams on his brakes or switches two or three lanes to avoid their attention, thereby drawing it and causing me to get pulled over for suspicious behavior. I'm always the "random" search on flights. I've been strip searched, pulled out of too many lines to count, and temporarily denied access to a few countries for acting "strangely". On our first *Nature Calls* shoot I somehow drove us onto a restricted military base in Arizona. I immediately started to panic, rambling to the confused guard about how we "were just looking for snakes", and acting, as our friend Colin described it, like a meth-head who was getting busted. This time, Dom suggested I pretend to be asleep.

My anxiety was rising as we got closer. "Don't swerve, you're swerving. They're going to think you're drunk"; "Please drive slower"; "Don't throw that apple core out the window! They can see you from here and will think you're trying to get rid of shit before the border!" When he pulled over within sight of the border agents to dump all of our garbage I almost lost my mind. There were multiple signs stating that all passengers must be awake and able to answer questions from the agents. Jarrod paid no mind and relaxed into the backseat. I was on high alert, though. I had our filming permit on my lap with my passport and driver's license, my snake stick was carefully hidden in the back, and I was nervously reciting a list of produce we had brought to snack on. Jarrod, half-asleep, looked up and said, "Hey, are fireworks cool in Canada? I brought a bunch of fireworks."

"Don't joke about that, man, seriously. Please," I pleaded.

"No, really, they're right here," answered a groggy and

completely calm Jarrod. "I thought they'd be fun on your birthday." He opened a brown paper bag and started pulling out bottle rockets, Roman candles, firecrackers, and more. My heart stopped beating. I felt all of the blood drain from my face. We were going to jail.

Dom, clearly the more level-headed one, said calmly, "That's awesome. Hahahha. Yeah, we probably shouldn't have those. Put them in a bag in the back, under some of our shit, out of sight."

Jarrod was still situating the bags after hiding the contraband when we pulled up to the drive-through inspection area. The officer peered down at us.

"How are you guys tonight?" he asked good-naturedly.

"Good, a little tired, but good," said Dom, as I stared forward out the window, not moving, sweating despite the freezing rain outside, and probably already looking like a terror suspect.

"Can I get all of your passports?" Dom passed them to the officer, whom I accidentally made eye contact with and went pale. "What brings you to Manitoba at this hour?"

"Just checking it out. Random road trip," said a confident, smiling, but clearly tired Dom.

"We're looking for snakes, sir!" I chimed in for no apparent reason from the passenger seat, suddenly staring at the officer with a huge stupid grin.

"What? Snakes? What do you mean?"

"Yeah, snakes!" I said, with far too much enthusiasm, as Jarrod stared openmouthed at me.

Dom just shook his head, muttering, "Jesus Christ, Pat, really?"

"I used to host a show for National Geographic, and we're filming a web-based wildlife series. There are amazing snakes in Manitoba!"

"So... you're filming a TV show? I'm confused. Will you be getting paid in Canada or the US?"

"Neither! We do it because it's what we love to do! We don't get paid!"

"Snakes?"

"Yeah! Red-sided garter snakes, mainly, but actually the dens are shared by every type of snake in the area! We may even find rattlesnakes!"

"So... you're filming a wildlife TV Show? Snake dens? Like, a gathering of snakes?"

Dom stepped in at that point, putting a hand in front of me. "No, no, we're hanging out, camping, hoping to find some animals that we can get some pictures and videos of. No big deal. This isn't a job, we're just hanging out."

"Please pull over and step out of the car."

"Absolutely," said a very tired-looking Dom. "Of course we'll do that now."

As Dom pulled away, a smiling Jarrod said, "What the fuck was that? I've never seen anything like that. Pat, what happened to you?"

"Oh that's just Pat's normal response when confronted with anyone in uniform," said Dom.

"That was *amazing*," grinned Jarrod.

We parked in front of empty-looking border offices and got out of the car, stretched, and grabbed our wallets and passports. Jarrod picked up his bright orange trucker hat with pictures of roosters on it, and we started towards the doors. They both kept looking at me and shaking their heads. I apologized, but was still on high alert.

"Please let me do the talking, if possible?" implored Dom. I hung my head. It was not possible. Once we got in the building, they separated the three of us in order to question us individually. I went into a lengthy explanation about the biological and geological anomaly that are the Narcisse Snake Dens. The guard didn't seem to believe to me, but after a Google search was amazed and wanted to know more. A further search turned up *Nature Calls*, then info on *Beast Hunter* and things were suddenly looking up. After about 10 minutes, Dom and I were both released into the general waiting area with our passports stamped. The guy searching our car walked in holding my snake stick with a concerned look on his face. The one who had questioned me intercepted him, showed him his computer screen, and suddenly I was getting lots of questions about snakes, bullet ants, and traveling. This was going well! Dom had sat down and was charging his iPhone. The guy had put the snake stick back and came back in to talk to us with no further searching of the car, still not really believing that there were pits with nearly 200,000 snakes just a couple hours away. Their main question was, why would we want to do this? Dom, exhaustedly deferred to me, saying, "It was his idea."

After another 10 minutes, we realized Jarrod had not joined us. "Where's your buddy? Is he still back there?" asked one of the guards, motioning to the room where Jarrod had been taken. "Let me see what's going on."

The guard came back a minute later, looking confused. "Sorry to say this, guys, but it looks like there's an outstanding warrant for your friend."

WHAT? Jarrod is many things – a felon is not one of them. He certainly isn't a felon who would make the stupid mistake of crossing a border. I'm not embarrassed to say that Jarrod is one of the best-looking people I know. Every time we mention him, Anna starts anything she's going to say with, "He's handsome" – which is the same reaction she has regarding Chris Evans and Brody Jenner. She isn't wrong. Jarrod is handsome. He has thoughtful blue eyes, curly and perpetually mussed blond hair, six-pack abs, and generally looks like he's just stepped out of an LL Bean catalogue. He, like Dom, is a supremely talented and accomplished artist. Descriptions of him alternate between "hipster" and "legit woodsman". When he is at his place in Jamaica Plain, the hipster label seems appropriate, but when you realize all of Jarrod's clothes are chosen based on his profession you see they are far more function than fashion, and just happen to be extremely fashionable on him. He also has a blonde mustache. He is the quietest of our group of friends and the most polite. He is comfortable in any situation, and will fit in perfectly anywhere. He's the type of guy who can talk to anyone, but he's also okay just observing everything going on around him. He doesn't drink, occasionally smokes American Spirits, and is absolutely the last person you would think would have an outstanding warrant.

"Do you know anything about this?" I asked Dom, all of my anxiety coming back.

"Nope," said Dom, without even looking up from his phone. "I'm sure it'll be fine. Jarrod can talk his way out of anything." Once again, Dom was not wrong. While my stomach was balling up in knots, it turns out Jarrod was laughing with his inquisitor about my snake comments while they waited for the matter to be sorted over the interwebs. It was all a big misunderstanding – there was no warrant, and his name had been flagged erroneously, or something along those lines. Jarrod didn't really need or get a full explanation, saying to the apologetic guards that it was all fine and sorted and that was all that mattered. He and his mustache were free to enter Canada. We received no questions about the fireworks so either they didn't find them, they didn't care about them, or they weren't illegal in the first place and I was just being super paranoid.

Dom and Jarrod continued teasing me as we left the station and piled back into my car. Jarrod offered to drive the rest of the way, and when I produced the stack of MapQuest directions and offered them to him, he and Dom looked at me like I'd just suggested we play Ariana Grande for the rest of the trip. Jarrod, kindly, just said, "No, man, that's okay, I've got it." I slumped into the backseat and promptly fell asleep.

I woke up to Dom and Jarrod screaming one of my many

nicknames given to me by a former boss based on my signature (P. Spain) and pulling me out of the car by my legs: "We're here! We're here! It's your motherfuckin' birthday, P Stain! PEEEEEE STAAAAAAAIN!!" – the last one delivered in a screaming, singsong voice.

And it was. It was my motherfuckin' birthday. It was about 4:30am and the sun was just appearing on the horizon in the parking lot of the Narcisse Snake Dens National Park. We were the only car in the gravel lot. More accurately, we were the only car for miles around. I picked myself off the ground, smiling groggily, and looked around. It was very cold, a little rainy, and extremely foggy. Not great snake weather. I climbed back into the car to grab a hoodie when Dom and Jarrod attacked me again.

"Open your presents!" Presents? I hadn't expected any presents. I felt like Harry Potter on his first Christmas morning at Hogwarts when Dom and Jarrod produced a piñata in the shape of a frog and told me to punch it while Jarrod held it. I was so sleepy that I almost punched Jarrod in the face on the first shot. They laughed and told me to hold it myself and punch it. I did, and it broke open, spilling its treasure.

There was a three foot, two pound gummy snake, a denim shirt (the "Canadian tuxedo"), some candy cigarettes, and various plastic jewelry and candy. We all laughed and tucked into a nutritious breakfast of chocolate chip cookies, bananas, PB and Js, and gummy snake. We then donned our matching Canadian tuxedos as we left the car to explore the snake dens and do our first reconnaissance of the area. John, our official Manitoba Government contact and guide, was going to meet us at 9am, so we had about four hours to ourselves.

We grabbed some filming gear and Dom started setting up to shoot while Jarrod took some production stills of me and the area. It's a really beautiful location – thousands of Aspens and short gnarled larch trees betray the swampy habitat around the dens, but give way to spruce and fir in the far distance. The forested areas were disrupted by large natural fields filled with grasses, grains, and the first signs of wildflowers. Even with the foggy, rainy, and freezing weather, I could tell right away that this was an absolutely perfect garter-snake habitat, and part of the reason why this spot has the largest concentration of snakes anywhere on earth. When the snakes emerge in the spring they are hungry and looking for love. Their hunger can be satiated easy enough in the surrounding swamps, which are filled with frogs, worms, slugs, and other tasty snake-treats. Likewise, their lust can be satisfied by the thousands of potential partners around.

This location in Manitoba really has a confluence of factors which make it perfect for these extreme numbers of snakes, however – a perfect serpentine storm, if you will. There is the food source, but a lot of places also have swampy regions with abundant food. There's the strategy of "den together, awake together, ORGY TIME!", but, again, this could happen anywhere. The main draw of *this* spot is a plethora of small, snake-sized tunnels that create easy access to underground limestone caves below the frost line. These are big enough for a snake, but too small for predators to enter and gorge themselves on the slow-moving reptiles. Without getting too dorky, and using broad, slightly inaccurate generalizations, snakes really can't regulate their body temperature, and rely on the environment to do it for them. Manitoba is about as far north as snakes can survive due to the frigid temperatures much of the year. A snake above the frost line would freeze and die over the winter. Denning together is a common over-winter strategy for a lot of snakes, but this far north it's essential. Also, the excessively large numbers of snakes raise the temperature in the den slightly – think strength/warmth in numbers. Just living produces a tiny amount of heat. Slight movements in their muscles, respiration, etc. all give off a nearly imperceptible amount of heat, even for a "cold-blooded" animal (I hate that term, but use it here to keep this explanation from becoming a book in and of itself). In an individual, this is insignificant; in 100,000 individuals, it is not. Cramming the limestone caves with snakes also regulates the temperature a little. Think about your fridge – it is most efficient when it is full, even if it's just full of water. Why? Because once the "stuff" in there reaches the set temperature, it stays there even when you open and close the door. If there's no "stuff" in there, the air reaches the set temperature but as soon as you open the door the air leaves and the "new" air has to be cooled. "Stuff" (such as snakes) maintain temperatures better than air.

All of these factors lead every snake within five to 10 square miles of the dens to return each year to this over-winter spot and partake in the ensuing orgy in the spring. The natural features draw the snakes, and the snakes draw the nerds, and the nerds bring their camera equipment. Anytime I saw Jarrod adopt his signature photographer pose I would freeze and give my "hero pose". This must have looked pretty funny to anyone else, if there was anyone within 50 miles, of course – Jarrod, feet and knees tight together, squatting with his entire lower body turned to the side and butt sticking way out, pointing the camera with an awkward two-handed grip at me, standing with my feet shoulder-width apart, hands at my sides, looking off into the distance with my chin jutting slightly out. It felt good to be doing this again. There's no reason in normal life to adopt this pose, and something about it made me remember what it was like to be a nature-show host – the slight absurdity of it, maybe.

Once Dom had the gear sorted we decided to check out the dens. The furthest is about a 15-minute walk from the parking area over beautiful, well-maintained trails. We were all excited when we spotted our first snake after about five minutes. It was definitely a red-sided garter snake, and was definitely not happy about being above ground. It was moving slow – so slow that, when Jarrod picked it up, it didn't change position at all, maintaining the stretched "S" curves of a snake on the move. It was almost as if it was frozen. When I held it I realized this was not far from the truth. I'd never felt a snake that cold. I held him in my warm hands for a couple minutes before he really started moving, then we put him down and got a few pictures of him before continuing on our way. The frozen snake was not raising my confidence that we were approaching the writhing mass of serpents I had envisioned.

I knew from speaking with John over e-mail for the past few weeks that, of the four dens, only two were likely to be "very active", although a warm spell the previous weekend had raised my hopes for a third. The first and smallest of the dens was empty. The dens are steep-sided indentations in the ground anywhere from five to about 20 feet below the path. They are fenced off to discourage people from walking into them and harming the snakes. The bottoms of the pits are covered in large stones, making them appear almost like a dry riverbed. The smallest is probably 5x5 and the largest is about 15x15, with the others somewhere in between.

The second and third both had a few very slow, very cold snakes slithering up their sides or lazily making their way around the bottom of the pits, appearing to be either hungover or really confused as to why they were there. The fourth and largest den site was also the one that John had said was our most promising prospect. We arrived at the overlook with high hopes and saw snakes. A lot of snakes, actually. More snakes than I had ever seen at once in my life, but not the flood of serpents I had expected. There were between 200-300 red-sided garter snakes slithering around in this stone-lined pit, which was about the size of your average living room. There appeared to be a lot more just below the rocks. These snakes, like the stragglers at the other dens, were moving pretty slow.

A larger concern than the poor showing of snakes was the

massive amount of very expensive video equipment set up in the den. There was a crane, a bunch of lights, a generator, and various odds and ends that demonstrated a professional film crew had beaten us to the action. For the sake of comparison, we were armed with two professional Canon cameras, one hobby-level one, and a couple of GoPros. Possibly, we'd be outgunned here. John had been very kind in giving us permission to film, but also very upfront about having a first-come-first-serve policy for filming the dens, and told me another crew might be there. In his words: "It's a big British production company, I don't know too many details." My hope was that at least two dens would be active so we wouldn't get in each other's way, but it was looking like we'd both be going for the same shot.

We considered stealing their equipment and leaving – this would have certainly made the trip fiscally worthwhile and upped the production value of our next project exponentially. After rejecting the idea based on the argument, "Pat will never be able to keep it together when we cross the border," plus some moral qualms, we decided we'd just reason with these unknown Brits. Surely they'd understand and clear out for the short amount of time we'd need to film, right?

Not wanting to waste any time, we jumped down into the pit, framed a few shots to avoid the equipment, and filmed a few pieces to camera about the pits. I caught about 50 snakes, Jarrod picked up handfuls of them, and Dom worked on getting good angles from above, in the pit, snake POV, etc. After about 25 minutes of filming, we noticed we had an audience.

It was just after 6am and we were standing in a light mist of freezing rain in an active snake den in Manitoba, so if I was to make a list of things we *didn't* expect to see, an attractive young Latina woman in skinny jeans, high-heeled boots, and a form-fitting parka would have been near the top. The bundled-up, tall, pale, bearded, and sullen-looking Canadian man with her seemed appropriate, though. When they noticed us looking up at them, the small woman started clapping, and waving to us.

"Hola! Hola! Hello! What are you doing down there? Do you love sneaks? Sneaks are interesting, but I am scared! I am Gaby of Manta, Ecuador! Who are you young handsome men? We are *so* quiet to not interrupt your cameras! I am Gaby, of Manta, Ecuador! Gaby like gabbing, talking! Yes? Brock! Brock! Introduce yourself to young handsome men! Brock! Brock! You say no one will be here and maybe no sneaks, but I say adventure finds us! Brock! Brock! See their cameras! Oh *sneak* adventure!"

Dom, Jarrod, and I looked at each other, unable to process this new development so early in the morning. Gaby of Manta, Ecuador? Brock? So many implied exclamation marks and so much excitement. What was happening? She was pulling on Brock's heavy-coated arm like an overexcited child – he looked about three feet taller than her – and literally jumping with joy. It was clear that, now we'd noticed them, they weren't going to keep quiet and allow us to continue filming. We were hoping that, as the sun rose, more snakes would show, so determined to come back in a couple hours. We wrapped it up and hiked up the steep sides of the den to meet our new superfan and her dour companion.

We greeted the very enthusiastic Gaby and less-than-thrilled Brock. The details of Gaby and Brock's relationship were hazy, at best. Was this a 90-day-fiancé situation? Were they married? Dating, even? All of this was very unclear. What was certain was that Gaby was from Manta, Ecuador – she stated this nearly every time she spoke – and *loving* Canada. Brock had been showing her all of the sights for the past two weeks, ever since she arrived from Manta, Ecuador. It was also clear that Brock was into her, and that she was into Dom.

While we walked back to the car, she kept telling us how handsome we all were, but Dom especially. She asked if she could touch Jarrod's mustache, and when he agreed she giggled and rubbed her fingers along his upper lip in a very provocative way and said, "Mmmmm," then licked her lips. Brock scowled. She then asked to rub my head and, when I consented, declared, "I don't like that too much. Brock, you should not shave your hair like this man, you *should* grow a mustache like this one, and hair like *this* one! Oh, the Dom! I love the long hair and look at your scruffy face! So handsome! So rugged!" She also declared that she loved blondes (Brock had dark hair and scowled again at this), then decided to "rate" the three of us.

She started with Jarrod: "Oh, you are so strong! I feel your muscles and your mustache reminds me of strong men in Ecuador. Your eyes are beautiful blue and your curly blonde hair is soft like a woman's. I think you are *very* handsome. Hug me!" She then abruptly wrapped her arms around a bemused Jarrod.

She then moved on to me: "Oh, you are the TV man! Nat Geo! Big man. No mustache, I don't like your face hair, your face is nice, though your arms are skinny, and I don't like your hair. I like your cheeks – strong good cheeks, very pretty face, handsome man, but the rest of you, eh," and made a "so-so" motion with her hand. Fair enough. Compared to Jarrod, that seemed like a good assessment.

Then she moved on to Dom: "Oh, the Dom! You have beautiful woman's hair and your face is so rugged! I love your rings and necklaces! Can I have one?"

"Absolutely not," said a very tired, less-than-amused Dom.

"Oh and strong! Strong-willed, too! You I like, you are so handsome! Can I sit in your car with you?"

"What? No, you can't sit in our car."

"Oh! You I like! You are my favorite, the most handsome, mystery man!"

Dom seemed a little flattered, but mostly confused and tired. He kept looking at Brock, who was smiling an unhappy smile that was more of a sneer. We walked a little in silence, and Brock and I started talking camera gear. He had a Nikon SLR and some high-end video equipment. He said that he and Gaby had been "making movies" together for the last two weeks. Again, there was a lot of implication in the way he said this, but we were reluctant to ask any more about either of them, and just let an awkward silence fall.

We got back to the parking lot and Gaby again rubbed Jarrod's mustache, my head, ran her fingers through Dom's feminine hair, then invited him – specifically not Jarrod or myself – over to Brock's place, which may or may not have been a hotel. We weren't very clear on the location. Dom declined, and Gaby and Brock left in a Dodge Charger, with Gaby leaning out the window blowing kisses.

"You just lost your chance at a threesome with them. You know that, right?" Jarrod said to Dom.

"Oh, I know, and I'm 100% fine with it."

We had a lot of questions that we couldn't answer: "What *was* that? Were they a couple? Why were they at the snake dens at 6am in the rain? Do you think Brock could have beaten us up? What are the chances that he had a gun? How do you think they met? What movies have they been making?" The mystery of Gaby and Brock lingered, questions never to be answered. I received an e-mail from her about a month later which did not clear up any of those mysteries. It did confirm that Gaby, was from Manta, Ecuador — two times in the short letter — and that the day we met was not a good day for sneaks, but was a good day for chatting.

In Gaby and Brock's absence we were once again alone in the parking lot, and exhaustion had kicked in. We still had a couple hours until John was scheduled to meet us, so we decided to take a nap. Dom grabbed the backseat, I took the front, and Jarrod stretched out on a nearby picnic table. I instantly fell asleep and woke up after what seemed like 10 seconds to the sound of children playing. A few more cars had pulled up and there were three or four small families milling around, putting juice boxes and granola bars into backpacks and getting ready for the 15 minute walk to the dens. Dom and Jarrod also woke up. It had stopped raining, but was still pretty cold and overcast. We ate some breakfast and waited for our official government guide.

John pulled into the parking lot in a huge Ford truck a few minutes later. He was a nice guy, probably late 40s, salt-and-pepper hair, muscular physique and angled face. Gaby would not have liked him. He shook our hands, made some small talk about the trip and offered to give us a tour of the dens. On the way he showed us the area where we could camp in, and we thanked him profusely. The first two den sites were still empty; the third had a few snakes slithering around, and the fourth was slightly more active than when we had been there hours before.

"Not a great day for snakes, eh?" said John.

"Well, hopefully it will clear up."

"Nope, not today, storm's coming in. Hate to tell you this with how far you drove, but it might be a washout." My face fell, and John must have noticed: "You never really can tell though, eh. This time of year the weather is pretty unpredictable, and weathermen just guess, if you ask me." I thanked him for the optimism.

While he explained all about the geology of the area and biology of the snakes his passion for this bizarre site was apparent, but when I asked him if he'd tell the camera what he just told me, he humbly replied, "Nah, I'd rather not. I'll let you guys do that stuff, eh." It was nice to meet a guy who promotes his work without promoting himself. He told us the other camera crew were "real nice guys", and was sure we could work with them to get the shots we wanted, as long as the weather cooperated. It would have been great to get him on camera because he was a wealth of knowledge about the dens, but also because he had a tendency to use the term "hemipene" when describing a snake's penis – which he did a lot. The snakes were there for some loving, after all. John used the term as only a seasoned biologist can – one who has gotten over the childlike joy in hearing a figure of authority say "hemipene" over and over. In his defense, a hemipenis is scientifically accurate, and "hemipene" is an accepted abbreviation, but both are slightly unnecessary for the general public, who don't really understand scientific descriptions of sexual attributes or characteristics.

We spent a few hours together, but it was clear the weather just wasn't on our side. John had a suggestion – there was a, strictly speaking, off-limits to the public quarry a few miles away that most people didn't know about, but actually had *more* snake activity than the "official" dens in recent years. Were we interested in checking it out? We absolutely were. We hopped into my car and raced behind John as he floored it down the deserted highway past gorgeous old farmhouses, crumbling barns, and rusted tractors displayed majestically on the edges of corn, wheat, and soy fields, with some shiny new modern farming equipment tucked into sheds and other shelters. It was like this region was struggling over what face to put forward – modern Central Canada, or a clearly well-loved and prosperous past. It reminded me of a prettier Nebraska, and that's not an easy thing to accomplish.

After about 15-20 minutes, John abruptly turned down a dirt path cut into the dense forest on one side of the road. There were a couple dozen of these turnoffs, all with chained "No Trespassing" signs spanning their narrow width. John removed the chain and invited us to follow him. We drove for another 15 minutes or so over rough terrain which my Scion was clearly not built for. By the time we reached a large clearing my shocks were groaning, a "check tires" light had lit up on my dash, and I had scraped one side of the car against some low-hanging branches. We stepped out of the beaten-up car into the brilliant noontime sun of a spring day in Central Canada.

After shielding my eyes from the unexpected and very welcome sunlight, my other senses starting kicking in.

Something seemed very odd here and I couldn't immediately put my finger on it. I could hear some birdsong, but there was an undercurrent of some unearthly noise that was echoing off the walls of the quarry and seemed to completely encompass the area. It was so pervasive, so insidious, that it was easy to miss at first. It was like the hum of an electric light, but off in some way. You could almost mistake it for the wind but for its consistency. In fact, it was the rustle-slither sound of tens of thousands of snakes crawling over each other. It's nearly indescribable in its strangeness.

After that sunk in, I noticed a smell. Anyone who's worked with reptiles in the wild or captivity can tell you they have a particular odor. It's musky but there's a faint hint of ammonia that you almost taste rather than smell, with a forward-facing hormonal scent that's kind of a mix of blood, skunk, and old seafood. There's also an undertone of earthy dust that's not entirely unpleasant. Some of the best reptile trackers I've known find their quarry using their noses. It's fun to be walking through the desert with them when you both suddenly perk up your noses, and wordlessly veer off the trail. There was nothing faint about this smell. It punched you in the face immediately and kept coming. Then there was the sight of a writhing blanket of snakes in front of us. There were a few fist-sized holes in the ground with snakes literally pouring out of them; snakes forming massive mating balls (one female with dozens of males trying to get with her) that would swell to such an uncontrollable size they would roll down the hill, lone individuals falling off in the ensuing mayhem, with confused, lost, or otherwise genetically inferior snakes climbing trees and weighing down the branches of saplings; snakes literally everywhere.

John saw the awed expressions on our faces, smiled, and said: "I think you guys can take it from here. Any questions, here's my cell. Make yourselves at home and I'm excited to see the video you come up with." I could barely speak as I shook his hand, thanking him again. This was better than I'd ever expected. We got down to filming right away, but struggled with exactly WHAT to film – everywhere we turned there were new sights: snakes falling from trees, huge females in the center of mating balls with dozens of males rubbing up on them and trying to earn the right to mate, snakes rolling down hills, snakes flowing like a river, snakes scattering beneath our feet as we walked, snakes appearing like a living carpet, snakes trying to climb us – it was a reptile nerd's dream.

We spent the afternoon reshooting everything we'd done in the snake dens that morning. This footage was far superior. By about four it seemed like we'd gotten everything we needed, and we were getting hungry. We decided to head back to the "real" dens and see if any activity had picked up there. That was a better-looking location, and we decided we'd splice together the shots and make it look like one location in the end, if the weather would cooperate and give us some continuity.

After another car-destroying trek to the highway, we were on the road in high spirits, heading back to the dens. After closing the windows on the highway due to a defect in my car that caused an ear-splitting bass rumble at speeds over 45, we realized just how bad we all smelled. We had spent four hours covered – COVERED – in snakes. The cloth seats in my car would never be the same. (In fact, after arriving back in Boston, my car was in such rough shape and smelled so bad that I sold it within a week. The dealer climbed in to check the mileage and, after an uncomfortable silence and making a few odd expressions, asked, "There seems to be an... unusual smell. It's really odd. Any idea what that's from?" I replied that I had no idea what he meant, and acted a little offended.)

We talked excitedly about what we had just witnessed. It was surreal. None of us could really wrap our heads around it. "Why don't more people know about this?" was the main question we kept coming back to. Why isn't this a tourist spot, and "snake island" in Japan is? Why can't I get a fridge magnet with "I survived the Narcisse Snake Dens"? Were the three of us really that different from the general population? This was AMAZING! One of the coolest things I have ever seen! Who *wouldn't* want to see this? As we pulled into the parking lot, Dom said: "If driving 36 hours each way to lie down in the world's largest pit of snakes doesn't sound like fun to you, then I don't think we can be friends." He spoke for all of us.

Back at the "real" den site, the weather was still overcast and cold, despite being less than an hour from the quarry, but the activity had picked up a little. We decided we'd already gotten all of the snake shots we needed, but filmed some intros, cutaways, B-roll, and cleanup shots that we'd talked about in the car. We had started roughing out a basic idea of what the finished video would look like based on what we'd filmed. We also came up with a shot list of footage that we needed to get that evening, the next day, and on the return trip.

Feeling pretty good, we walked over to the furthest den and saw the rival film crew, which consisted of two very tired-looking guys who were a little older than us. We started to introduce ourselves and, to my great shock, one of them asked, "Are you Pat Spain from Icon Films?" I admitted that I was. Amazingly, they were from Bristol in England, and were good friends with Barny and the others from the Icon crew! They were at the dens for three weeks filming the big-budget *Wild Canada* for the BBC. They said they had some great footage of the dens, but were hoping to get better shots in the coming week as they were predicting record-breaking warm temperatures a couple days later. They said they could clear a space for us the next day so we could shoot anything we needed if there was any good activity. They encouraged us to stick around for an extra week, saying they knew we could get some amazing footage. We told them about the quarry, but they said they needed to stay at the den sites because of their permits and the cinematic value of the surrounding area. A human-made quarry just wouldn't cut it for the Big Brown Cow (aka BBC). Luckily for *Nature Calls*, we had no such constraints. What we did have constraints on was time – we needed to leave the next day, regardless of what we'd filmed or not. We were happy with the footage we'd gotten, and, despite the promise of a pit filled five-feet deep with snakes, we couldn't stick around.

We told the guys we were planning to camp out and, knowing the joy of a bed after a long trip, they told us about a hotel in town that wouldn't break the bank and recommended a restaurant nearby for "local delicacies". They were right. We'd earned a nice night out in whatever town we were closest to. It was my birthday, after all, and it would be nice to have a good meal and a night's sleep on a real bed. We decided to follow their advice and drive the hour or so into town, or rather, the "Rural Municipality of Gimli in the Heart of New Iceland".

Gimli, we found out, is not just the dwarf from LOTR, but also a small town on the shore of beautiful Lake Winnipeg, whose residents are not amused when asked, "Certainty of death? Small chance of success? What are we waiting for?" The main tourist attraction there is a 15-foot statue of a Viking, and there isn't much else to say about a place where the main tourist attraction is a statue of a Viking. This Viking also graces the only Gimli fridge magnet available, just as an FYI. Joking aside it was a very nice little town, and I could see it being a good family vacation spot in the summer, but in early May it was practically a ghost town.

We checked into our three-person room, ate some delicious pickerel and drank Canadian beers at the Beach Boy restaurant, as recommended by the BBC crew, and enjoyed some disturbingly named "fudge-buster" donuts at Robins for dessert. Jarrod and Dom decided to jump in Lake Winnipeg, despite the freezing temperatures, and I opted for a more traditional way to rinse-the-snake-stink-off via our hotel shower. Refreshed, we remembered a bar we'd passed on the way to the hotel, and Dom and Jarrod said it was their duty to buy me a birthday whiskey.

We laughed about the adventures of the past couple days and continued theorizing about Gaby and Brock as we drove towards the sketchy-looking bar we'd passed. It was only about 7:30 and everything in Gimli appeared to be closed. We weren't holding out high hopes, but thought that, if anything opened "late" on a Wednesday night in this town, it was the grimy-looking biker bar. We were not disappointed. Not only was the bar open, but it turned out Wednesday nights were special at this "Bar and Lounge".

The bar looked more like an American Legion than a "bar and lounge", and was completely empty aside from us, an older female bartender with very tall dyed red hair, a bouncer/ ID checker who looked like he would be able to tell a *lot* of interesting stories about methamphetamines, and a couple of old, leather-clad, bearded men who appeared to work there in some capacity. We strolled in and took in the ambiance. Stained, oddly-colored, cigarette-burned Berber rug? Yup, they had it. Mismatched tables and folding chairs? Check. A very unusual, hard to place, omnipresent, unpleasant smell? It was rife with it. How about a bartender behind bulletproof glass? Glad you asked – yes, and this was a first for me. They also had old, mismatched couches, lazy boys and, bizarrely, a very well-advertised VIP section.

Dom went to the "bar" – actually a recessed room separated from the main space by the aforementioned bulletproof glass. Drinks were served, much like scratch tickets at a Bodega, under the glass, and ordered through tiny holes cut at mouth level. I've been to quite a few bars all over the world – from hole-in-the-wall places in the Congo to Michelin-starred spots in Barcelona – and consider myself fairly well versed in alcohol varietals. The only booze I recognized behind that glass was Jack Daniels. Everything else was either a generic "spirit" labeled much like all of the drinks in *Repo Man* – "vodka" in a black-on-white label, "whiskey" in a white-on-black label, etc. – or some terrible-looking, hangover inducing, sickeningly-sweet liqueur. Dom opted for the unknown "whiskey" – which was an interesting call. Our "shots", and Jarrod's Coke, were large cups of brownish liquid on the rocks served in red Solo cups, and priced at $4 US.

As we were toasting my surviving another year, our adventure, and the snakes, the very intimidating leather-clad bouncer approached and asked if we'd be staying for the strip club – because, if so, he had to charge us a $5 cover, but, being that it was my birthday, he'd waive the fee for me. Excuse me? Strip club? We looked around us. "Here?" we asked.

"Yeah. This bar turns into a strip club every Wednesday night at 9." I looked around again. There was no stage, no lights, and no sound system other than an old CD player on a folding chair in one corner. Now, I have to admit that I've never been to a strip club, but this was not what I imagined them to look like. Dom and Jarrod are somewhat connoisseurs of gentlemen's clubs throughout the lower 48, but looked equally confused.

"Where do they strip?" was about all I could think to ask.

"Right around here, you know. These couches and chairs you all are in."

"Are there a lot of dancers?"

"A few. You've gotta hang around to find out, I guess."

The VIP area and smell suddenly seemed a little more disturbing. I didn't think this should be my first strip-club experience – despite Dom and Jarrod's insistence that this was *exactly* what my first strip-club experience should be – and decided we would not be hanging out until 9. Don't get me wrong, I'm not a prude and have no inherent moral issue with strip clubs – a good friend of mine in college made all of her tuition for a four-year private college by stripping for six months, and a friend from Icon did a documentary on exotic dancers which required him to hang out at a club every day for months and then take a bunch of the ladies on their first trip abroad, making him some lifelong friends. I've just never been to one. The main reason for this is that I'm a complete nerd. It's nearly impossible to embarrass me, and just about the only way to make me uncomfortable is to flirt with me. I get extremely tongue-tied, trip over myself, literally and figuratively, and find the entire experience wholly awkward and frustrating. It took me years to ask Anna out on a date, despite us being friends for the duration. The idea of a naked woman flirting with me sounds more terrifyingly awful than titillating.

Dom and Jarrod protested, but then thought about my personality for a minute and agreed that it made sense, and it was my birthday after all. And for my birthday I wanted to catch snakes, so, catch snakes we would. We said goodbye to the weirdest bar I've ever visited after another drink, and went back to the hotel where we would wake up early the next day, have some more fudge-busters, and head back to the snake dens.

Bright and early the next morning, we were refreshed, filled with caffeine and chocolate, and ready for the snakes. This time the weather seemed to be on our side. As we started walking towards the pit we heard that now familiar rustling sound and all started grinning. The smell hit us next, and we quickened our pace. By the time we got near the 4th den we knew we were going to be walking into something incredible. I'd estimate the pit was about 50% active, based on other footage I've seen and folks I've spoken with who are familiar with the site. There were thousands of snakes, too many to estimate, writhing and mating, climbing up the sides of the pit and forming those rivers and rolling balls of snakes we'd seen the day before in the quarry, but in a much smaller, more concentrated area, so it was easier to be overwhelmed by the strangeness of it.

We stood transfixed for a couple minutes just watching, listening, and smelling. Jarrod then said, "So, are you going down in there, or what?"

"Of COURSE I am!" I said. I did a piece to camera as I scrambled down the ledge. I laughed as I scooped up my first armful of snakes, realizing I could reach down almost to my elbow before I touched rock in spots.

Larger rocks sticking out of the flowing river of snakes allowed Dom and I to carefully hop our way to the very center while Jarrod filmed from above. I reached into the mass with both arms, scooping up dozens of snakes and letting them slide through my hands and arms. They covered my boots as the tide rose and overtook some of the lower rocks we'd been standing on. Their numbers swelled from beneath us as more and more emerged from their underground den. I was giddy. Dom was enjoying himself, but every once in a while would smell his hands or clothes and mutter "gross" under his breath. Jarrod seemed to be in stunned silence. The thermometer and swell of snakes rose with the sun, and most of the rocks were overtaken by noon. Amazingly, this was only 70% active according to John, who had returned to see how we were doing. The BBC film crew had returned and, true to their word, made sure we'd gotten all of the footage we needed before they started setting up their equipment again. We had more than enough, and were already dreading the massive editing job we had ahead of us, so we decided to just enjoy the last couple of hours and put the equipment away.

The last shot we got was the one I had spoken with Dom and Jarrod about when pitching this trip. I carefully cleared a sunny spot to lie down in on one of the rocks, sunk my arms under the blanket of snakes, and lifted a few dozen onto myself. Within minutes, they were climbing all over me. As Dom and Jarrod filmed, I laughed – at the absurdity of it, at the insanity and weirdness. Then the darker thoughts came. The questions of why I was doing this, the uncertainty about the future, the guilt about the past year – it hit me again. Once the snakes started making their way up my pant legs, I decided we had the shot and pushed the thoughts to the back of my mind.

Dom and Jarrod then joined me in the pit. They both jumped right in, figuratively speaking – literally, they tiptoed in, so as to not crush hundreds of snakes beneath their feet. They started grabbing armfuls of snakes, taking pictures of each other with their iPhones, laughing, and just basking in the sheer absurdity of it all. By the time the BBC guys were set up we were ready to clamber up the sides of the pit and say goodbye to the snake dens. It was another life goal accomplished.

So, full disclosure – the "200,000 snakes" I started this book with is an impossible to determine number. No one site has that many snakes, but it was one of the estimates that I read of the entire "den" site. I've also read anywhere from 70,000 to 400,000. Some say the entire population of the Narcisse sites – the park, the quarry, and other hotspots – comes to over half a million. Whatever the truth is, it's a lot of snakes. An unimaginable number. Did I lie down in 200,000 snakes? Who knows. Probably not. It could have been more or less. It was a living sea of snakes, multiple feet deep at numerous points. I personally interacted with over a thousand snakes that day, by my estimate – the scent of my clothes and car would corroborate.

On our way out of the park we saw a few dozen schoolkids on a field trip. I caught a few snakes that had left the pit, starting their summer migration throughout Manitoba, and gave an impromptu talk about snake biology. The kids and teachers were having a great time, and so was I. It reminded me why I'd started all of this wildlife show stuff to begin with. I love teaching, and I love getting people as excited about animals and nature as I am. TV was a means to an end – reaching the largest audience and getting them to care about the animals I love. This hands-on presentation and the smiles on the kids' and teachers' faces brought it all back. They asked questions, I taught them to hold snakes properly without hurting the animal, and they loved it. Some of these kids had never even seen a snake up close, much less held one before this! They all wanted their teachers to take pictures of them holding or touching a snake. Some kids who were freaked out at first started catching them on their own. Others petted little garter snakes and cooed to them like they would a puppy. It was incredible. It reminded me that, behind all of the corporate politics, network instability, wardrobe decisions, executive meetings, and travel frustrations, was this – education, changing people's attitudes about animals. Getting people to care about them and potentially changing their lives and removing fears. It was on this high note that the three of us jumped back in the car and headed to Boston.

The ride back was fun, but more low-key, as rides home tend to be. I let Dom do all of the talking at the border and we sailed through. We joked around about the smell, about killing my car, and kept coming back to the absurdity of what we had just done. We were getting hungry as we passed Fargo, North Dakota, and decided that was as a good a spot as any to stop and grab a bite. We drove past some pubs and settled on Rick's Bar, which had a giant neon cowboy boot advertising "food". After parking and seeing some rough-looking characters exiting the establishment, I decided to Yelp it. Reviews seemed to revolve around a "general feeling of being unsafe" or "fights broke out all around me". I decided this was not a good way to end the trip. While Dom and Jarrod could have played it cool, I know myself well enough to understand that this was not a spot for me. We drove on until we passed The Turf, which looked like a college pub and restaurant. Their sign indicated a special on buffalo burgers and "Ice-hole" shots. Done and done.

Right as we walked in we knew we'd made the right decision. The place was packed with a good mix of locals and college kids, indie rock was playing on the sound system, and the bartenders were laughing and not wearing flare, nor were they behind bulletproof glass. We all ordered various buffalo burgers and a

$5 pitcher of beer ($4 refills!). Before the friendly young waitress left she shocked us by asking, "Are you Pat Spain from National Geographic?" Despite what some people may believe, I do not get recognized by general members of the TV-viewing public often, and can count on one hand the number of times it has happened, so was convinced Dom or Jarrod had put her up to it.

"Ha, ha, very funny, guys. I'm sorry about them, they like to joke around."

"No, really, are you?"

Dom and Jarrod both swore they had nothing to do with it, but grinned, excited to see what would happen here.

"He is," said Jarrod. "We're his crew. We just had a new adventure up north."

"NO WAY! Are you really? Guys! This guy is on National Geographic and he's just finished filming something!"

More bartenders and wait staff came over to the table. Free drinks were poured, we took a bunch of pictures with the staff, autographs were signed, selfies were posted on social-media sites, and stories started flowing like ice-holes. After a while I was pretty full on free appetizers, and pretty drunk. Everyone was laughing at our stories. They wanted to hear about where we had just been, then they wanted to smell us, and things just got messy and fun after that. Jarrod was the designated driver so, after a few hours, it was his thankless duty to let us know that we'd better hit the road. We hugged everyone, took a few more pictures, and went back to my defiled and barely functioning car.

I was a little too drunk to truly notice it in Fargo but, by the time we reached somewhere around Toledo, Ohio, when I was having my 5th coffee and nursing my headache as I prepared to take my first shift behind the wheel since leaving The Turf 14 hours earlier, I had an epiphany. It wasn't until that bar in Fargo that I really knew I was back. Forget social media, my insecurities, my day job, responsible finances, this lifetime of scans and tests I have in front of me, and the stats that gave me a 50% chance of living, and most of all *fucking* cancer – none of that matters when you're doing the things you really love and living the life you are meant to live.

I honestly have the greatest partner in Anna, the best friends in the world, an amazing family, remarkable kids, and the only life I will ever want. Whether I ever do another episode of TV or not, I realized in that bar that I will always be doing *this*. This was not the end because I will always be learning about and experiencing new things – things that, in that moment, I didn't know about, so couldn't be added to some list. Adding my family to these adventures opens up possibilities for experiences I could never dream of! My goal? My goal was then, and is now, to experience all of the absurdity that I can, because life IS absurd. Life is amazing and overwhelming and stupid and wonderful. Life is a pit of snakes, and kids vomiting on you at 2am, and a volcano lake in Sumatra at sunrise, and a man you've just met trying to get you to follow him to his car so he can show you something about goats. It's everything, and everything that you make it.

It's okay that I'm alive and others are not. It's okay for me to love this life I've got however I want, even if other people think it's weird. It's okay to still be the exact same person I was before cancer in some ways, and completely different in others. It's okay to feel or think about things differently to before, or be unsure of how to think about them. It's okay to do absolutely anything for the people who helped me through this, even if they didn't know they were helping, and to do the same for the people who ran away because they were scared or couldn't handle it. It's okay that they couldn't handle it.

I will be going on ridiculous adventures with incredible people, experiencing things most people will only read about, getting others as excited about wildlife as I am, making my own path and loving every second of it. It made perfect sense that this was what I was doing one year after chemo, because it made absolutely no sense. And neither did cancer. And neither did getting and losing a TV show. None of it made sense because it was my life, and my life will never make sense. But it will always be my life, and I love it, and the people I love see it and love it also. I haven't felt guilty about my life since that day.

Thanks to Anna, Jarrod, Dom, a bar full of locals in Fargo, and nearly 200,000 snakes, I knew that I was still, and always will be, the Beast Hunter, and my story is far from over.

Acknowledgements

While I have dedicated this book to Anna, I truly could not have completed it without the help of many incredible people who I am so fortunate to have in my life. I'd like to take a minute to thank each of them.

Our kids, Luna Caulfield and Wallace Charles. The greatest aspect of my life is being a part of theirs.

My insane and wonderful family – Al, Mom, Sarah, and Nathan who have supported and encouraged me throughout my life. Mom, who learned more about alligator reproduction than she probably ever wanted to in her quest to support a budding young biologist, and Al who took me camping and fishing despite having no interest in these activities himself, which I never knew until I was in my late twenties. Sorry about child welfare having to come to the house and watch you change diapers and question Sarah about possible neglect/abuse after I got salmonella from a lizard, then spread it to about a dozen friends, and cracked my head open sledding, and sliced my legs open sliding down a hill to catch a snake – hopefully this makes up for the embarrassment?

The entire current and past Icon family, particularly Harry and Laura Marshall. Harry and Laura are two of my favorite people on Earth. They are the people Anna and I want to be when we grow up. They are the smartest, nicest, funniest, and most caring and loving people you could hope to meet, and the greatest thing about doing TV has been having them enter our lives. We love them like family. In addition to Harry and Laura there's Andie Clare, Lucy Middleboe, Stephen McQuillan, Barny Revill, James Bickersteth, Alex Holden, Anna Gol, Ben Roy, Laura Coates, Sol

Welch, Belinda Partridge, Abi Wrigley, Duncan Fairs, Robin Cox, Simon Reay, Brendan McGinty, and everyone else, who continue to be amazing forces of encouragement and support.

The Nat Geo team behind *Beast Hunter* – Janet Han Vissering, Steve Burns, Ashley Hoppin, Sydney Suissa, Russel Howard, Chris Albert, Geoff Daniels, Mike Mavretic, Dara Klatt, Steve Ashworth, Whit Higgins, and others. Thank you so much for your support and trust in allowing me to fulfill a lifelong dream, and letting Icon take the lead and make a series we are all really proud of.

The most amazing and supportive group of friends I could ask for – Adam Manning, Dom Pellegrino, Joe Viola, and Adrianna Wooden. Thank you for sticking by me and being there for me and my family through everything.

Thank you so much to the entire team at John Hunt Publishing, especially John Hunt, who saw the potential of the massive and messy manuscript I sent over, Dominic James, who assured all of my insecurities and answered all of my questions while reassuring me that it was all going to be okay, and the expert editing of Graham Clarke, who managed to pull these six books together and make them the cohesive series.

My very literary friends and family who served as the first reviewers of this book – Al Spain, Joe Viola, Dom Pellegrino, Richard Sugg, Sarah Franchi, Gene Campbell, Tim Fogarty, John Johnson, Zeb Schobernd, Sarahbeth Golden, and Luke Kirkland – thank you for your insights and mocking. This book is much better because of you.

The folks at my day job who have supported my insane extracurricular activities – especially Bill O'Connor who gave me the opportunity to do this and assured me I'd still have a job when I returned.

Thanks to all of the incredible fixers, guides, and translators who kept us alive and safe, often risking your own lives in the process.

The amazing physical therapists and teams of doctors who have kept me alive and mostly mobile all of these years, especially Popi, Bill and Nancy.

All of the folks from Stupid Cancer, the American Cancer Society, ACS CAN, Real Men Wear Pink, ASCRS, and RELAY. You all make a difference in people's lives.

All of the caregivers, survivors, and people dealing with cancer right now. Reach out to the orgs above – there is a community for you.

Thanks, finally, to the readers and fans of these shows! I hope you've enjoyed what you've seen and read! You can find all of my social media stuff at www.patspain.com. I try to answer questions and respond as best I can. Genuinely – thank you!

Continue the adventure with the Pat Spain On the Hunt Series

A Little Bigfoot: On the Hunt in Sumatra
Pat Spain lost a layer of skin, pulled leeches off his neither regions and was violated by an Orangutan for this book
Paperback: 978-1-78904-605-2
ebook: 978-1-78904-606-9

200,000 Snakes: On the Hunt in Manitoba
Pat Spain got and lost his dream job, survived stage 3 cancer, and laid down in a pit of 200,000 snakes for this book.
Paperback: 978-1-78904-648-9
ebook: 978-1-78904-649-6

A Living Dinosaur: On the Hunt in West Africa
Pat Spain was nearly thrown in a Cameroonian prison, learned to use a long-drop toilet while a village of pygmy children watched, and was deemed "too dirty to fly" for this book.
Paperback: 978-1-78904-656-4
ebook: 978-1-78904-657-1

A Bulletproof Ground Sloth: On the Hunt in Brazil
Pat Spain participated in the most extreme tribal ritual, accidentally smuggled weapons, and almost lost his mind in the Amazonian rainforest for this book.
Paperback: 978-1-78904-652-6
ebook: 978-1-78904-653-3

The Mongolian Death Worm: On the Hunt in the Gobi Desert
Pat Spain ingested toxic "foods", made a name for himself in traditional Mongolian wrestling, and experienced the worst bathroom on Earth for this book.
Paperback: 978-1-78904-650-2
ebook: 978-1-78904-651-9

Sea Serpents: On the Hunt in British Columbia
Pat Spain went to the bottom of the ocean, triggered a bunch of
very angry fisherman, and attempted to recreate an iconic scene
from Apocalypse Now for this book.

Paperback: 978-1-78904-654-0
ebook: 978-1-78904-655-7

I'm Still With You
True Stories of Healing Grief Through Spirit Communication
Carole J. Obley
A series of after-death spirit communications which uplift, comfort
and heal, and show how love helps us grieve.
Paperback: 978-1-84694-107-8 ebook: 978-1-84694-639-4

Less Incomplete
A Guide to Experiencing the Human Condition Beyond the
Physical Body
Sandie Gustus
Based on 40 years of scientific research, this book is a dynamic
guide to understanding life beyond the physical body.
Paperback: 978-1-84694-351-5 ebook: 978-1-84694-892-3

Advanced Psychic Development
Becky Walsh
Learn how to practise as a professional, contemporary spiritual
medium.
Paperback: 978-1-84694-062-0 ebook: 978-1-78099-941-8

Astral Projection Made Easy
and overcoming the fear of death
Stephanie June Sorrell
From the popular Made Easy series, *Astral Projection Made Easy*
helps to eliminate the fear of death, through discussion of life
beyond the physical body.
Paperback: 978-1-84694-611-0 ebook: 978-1-78099-225-9

The Miracle Workers Handbook
Seven Levels of Power and Manifestation of the Virgin Mary
Sherrie Dillard
Learn how to invoke the Virgin Mary's presence, communicate with her, receive her grace and miracles and become a miracle worker.
Paperback: 978-1-84694-920-3 ebook: 978-1-84694-921-0

Divine Guidance
The Answers You Need to Make Miracles
Stephanie J. King
Ask any question and the answer will be presented, like a direct line to higher realms... *Divine Guidance* helps you to regain control over your own journey through life.
Paperback: 978-1-78099-794-0 ebook: 978-1-78099-793-3

The End of Death
How Near-Death Experiences Prove the Afterlife
Admir Serrano
A compelling examination of the phenomena of Near-Death Experiences.
Paperback: 978-1-78279-233-8 ebook: 978-1-78279-232-1

Where After
Mariel Forde Clarke
A journey that will compel readers to view life after death in a completely different way.
Paperback: 978-1-78904-617-5 ebook: 978-1-78904-618-2

Harvest: The True Story of Alien Abduction
G L Davies
G. L. Davies's most terrifying investigation yet reveals one woman's terrifying ordeal of alien visitation, nightmarish visions and a prophecy of destruction on a scale never before seen in Pembrokeshire's peaceful history.
Paperback: 978-1-78904-385-3 ebook: 978-1-78904-386-0

The Scars of Eden
Paul Wallis
How do we distinguish between our ancestors' ideas of God and close encounters of an extra-terrestrial kind?
Paperback: 978-1-78904-852-0 ebook: 978-1-78904-853-7

Readers of ebooks can buy or view any of these bestsellers by clicking on the live link in the title. Most titles are published in paperback and as an ebook. Paperbacks are available in traditional bookshops. Both print and ebook formats are available online.
Find more titles and sign up to our readers' newsletter at http://www.johnhuntpublishing.com/mind-body-spirit.
Follow us on Facebook at https://www.facebook.com/OBooks and Twitter at https://twitter.com/obooks.